FORTHTELLING INNOVATION

SOARING
with

FAITH

The Difference Maker
for Congregations

GEORGE W. BULLARD JR.

Illustrated by Joe McKeever

𝕿𝕬𝕭
MEDIA GROUP

IRON
STREAM
MEDIA

Birmingham, Alabama

Soaring with Faith

TAB Media Group
Published in conjunction with Iron Stream Media
100 Missionary Ridge
Birmingham, AL 35242
IronStreamMedia.com

Some material in this book was first published in The Baptist Paper, both in print and online, and is reprinted with permission.

George continues to write regular columns for The Baptist Paper. To subscribe, visit thebaptistpaper.org or email subscribe@thebaptistpaper.org.

Library of Congress Control Number: 2026903170

Cover design by twolineSTUDIO.com

ISBN: 979-8-9934736-0-4 (paperback)
ISBN: 979-8-9934736-1-1 (eBook)

1 2 3 4 5—29 28 27 26 25

"Building on his 50-plus years of advising congregations, George offers great hope to leaders seeking to move their congregations into the new realities, contexts, and the call of God that is unique to each congregation. Thus, helping them soar in fulfilling God's mission. George continues to mentor not only me, but hundreds of other church leaders through his mentoring and writing. *Soaring with Faith: The Difference Maker for Congregations* is filled with live examples, practical tools, and paths for all churches, regardless of their tribe or tradition."

—DAVE TRAVIS, Strategic Consultant to Pastors and Church Boards at Generis. He was formerly the CEO of Leadership Network.

"George Bullard brings decades of proven wisdom to help congregations move beyond survival into Spirit-led vitality. He has always been a source of encouragement to me personally. His wisdom has shaped everything from local congregations to the Baptist World Alliance itself. With clarity, practical insight, and deep passion for the Church, this book calls leaders to embrace God's vision and to move from struggling and stumbling into courageously soaring with faith toward their full Kingdom potential. Read this if you're looking for a roadmap to faith-based leadership for your congregation."

—ELIJAH BROWN, General Secretary and CEO of Baptist World Alliance

"George Bullard is a refreshing combination of strategic thinking and Spirit-driven revelation. It is never more evident than who I know George to be. This kind of person is rare. It's the kind of person I want to be. It's the kind of person I long to have in the room with me. It's the kind of leader I believe is so necessary for the future of the Church. *Soaring with Faith* pulls you into the room with George. It challenges the kind of leader we need to become. His wit and wisdom are evident on every page."

—DAVE RHODES, Co-Founder of Clarity House and Strategic Director for the Grace Family of Churches, Atlanta, Georgia

"Congregational leaders long for clarity about the present and courage for the future. *Soaring with Faith* introduces typologies that help leaders see the needed shifts to step into their full Kingdom potential. George is a trusted, thought-provoking practitioner who loves King Jesus and His bride, revealing a rare blend of spiritualist and strategist. His insights are biblically grounded and shaped by decades of walking with scores of congregations. Prayerful readers will discover unseen barriers holding congregations back, along with hopeful pathways forward. This book is a gift for all who long to lead God's people with clarity, courage, and faith-filled vision."

—SHANE STACEY, Co-Founder of Clarity House and Congregational Consultant and Coach

"George Bullard shatters the unhelpful labels of 'healthy' or 'unhealthy' and gives churches a fresh, Spirit-led framework for true vitality and vibrancy. For the past five years, I've used his insights nearly every day—in coaching pastors, consulting with congregations, and guiding leaders toward their next step. This book is more than theory. It's a practical, transformative tool that equips pastors, church leaders, and denominational and network partners to reimagine ministry. Read it, wrestle with it, and you will discover a courageous path into God's preferred future."

—CHRIS REINOLDS, Associational Mission Strategist for Northeast Florida Baptist Association and Founder of The Reinolds Group

"George Bullard wants congregations to soar with faith! This book provides principles, real-life experiences, and solid solutions to ignite the same urgency in all congregational leaders. As George outlines so eloquently, our commitment must follow God's leading, not our personal preferences. George calls his commitment 'radical,' and the future of our congregations depends on us getting this right. My respect and gratitude for George's ministry and all his 'Bullard-isms' is based on his passion to help congregations 'know, feel, do, become, and fulfill all to which God is calling you.' And I say 'Amen' to that!"

—MARY ANN SIBLEY, Owner, Coach, Cheerleader at Matterspark.com

"*Soaring with Faith* is a well of wisdom. Decades of serving, leading, consulting, and coaching with congregations, denominations, and networks have given George an unusual vantage point for experiencing and understanding a broad spectrum of congregations—Spiritless to Soaring. Congregations do not have to accept mediocrity in their ministry or surrender to conformity and cultural captivity. Instead, George wants to help pull—not push—them toward the life-giving power of the Kingdom of God. This book is a demonstration of and an invitation to conversation, reflection, exploration, and inspiration. May the Holy Spirit help more of us to soar."

—David Emmanuel Goatley, President | Clifford L. Penner Presidential Chair | Professor of Theology & Ministry at Fuller Theological Seminary

"In an ephemeral world where instant gratification is too slow, George muscles a half-century of congregational learning and leading into a readable work that will help you put air under the wings of your congregation. If you wonder why you're plodding instead of soaring, George offers a helping hand to lift your fellowship toward realizing its full Kingdom potential."

—Norman Jameson, Christian journalist living the dream as a sheep herder in Pennsylvania

"As a fifty-year veteran serving congregations within an array of denominations, this gripping read reaffirms what George has become. Convincing credentials, coupled with amazing life experiences, bestows on today's congregations new wings upon which to soar. His writings clearly represent the pull of God rather than the push of humankind. His conversational tone entertainingly provides the reader with decades of research-based spiritual 'Aha!' moments. These assure clarity and alignment for congregations aspiring to participate in a future known only to God. This book truly is a cosmic wormhole to a different place in the universe, helping congregations rapidly accelerate and soar with faith."

—John Bost, Founder of Master Counsel in Winston-Salem, North Carolina, while along the way a city mayor, executive pastor, consultant/ coach, and author

"*Soaring with Faith* distills decades of George's ministry and consulting work into a framework that examines the life cycles churches experience as God pulls them toward His redemptive plan. If you are looking for a how-to book with simple solutions and silver bullets for church growth, then this book is not for you. George's deep and long-term experience and expertise give you the tools to think, evaluate, and lead wherever God has planted you."

—John Waters, Lead Pastor, First Baptist Church, Statesboro, Georgia

"*Soaring with Faith* provides American churches with a much-needed map through the modern evangelical landscape. Too many congregations today are declining, and leaders are often at a loss to understand their situation. Much less to bring about needed change. That's where George steps in. This book is unflinching in evaluating a congregation's true condition, but also hopeful in charting a new direction. It is a realistic but practical guide for leadership. Congregational leadership teams will reap great rewards in allowing George to speak into their congregations' present struggles as well as their future promise."

—MIKE TURNER, Pastor and Blogger at MTurner on Substack

"*Soaring with Faith* is an excellent resource for a comprehensive approach to transforming congregations. Some transformation-focused resources are only theory, paradigm shifts, or even technical suggestions that work in some congregations somewhere. George's extensive ministry with numerous congregations has become wisdom. It is church craft that will guide readers into actionable approaches to living into God's calling for their congregations. This book realistically recognizes the challenges inherent in being church in this century, while standing firm on the unwavering hope energizing and sustaining congregations when they are in Christ. *Soaring With Faith* will stretch your thinking while firing your spiritual imagination."

—MARK E. TIDSWORTH, Founder and Team Leader, Pinnacle Leadership Associates

"George has been my mentor, colleague, and friend throughout my ministry. *Soaring with Faith* is a culmination of his wisdom and insights as he comes alongside congregations to help them discover God's vision and direction. He uses an exceptional consulting approach flavored with a coaching mindset to help congregations discover the steps to take by faith into God's future for them. George is one of the most innovative church practitioners I know. This book will assist pastors, congregational leaders, and denominational staff in a process that builds a foundation for fresh discoveries and a visionary path for the future."

—KEN KESSLER, Coaching and Networking Director with Baptists in Virginia

I dedicate this book to three groups of people ...

Thanks for the mentoring
Lyle Schaller
Larry McSwain
Willis Bennett
Russell Bennett
Lawrence Childs
Don Hammer
Jere Allen

Thanks for the collegial relationships
Glenn Akins
Ken Kessler
Chris Reinolds

Thanks for taking care of essential administrative things so I
had time to learn the things I am sharing
Irene Featheringill
Laura Settle
Elaine Kessler

Table of Contents

Read This First!

The first thing you may want to know is, what does it mean to *Soar with Faith* and to be *The Difference Maker for Congregations*?

I get it. I would want a brief summary before I buy, borrow, or invest time in reading this book. I am delighted to offer you the same consideration.

Soaring with Faith is about five sets of Protestant Christian congregations in North America, which I call collectives: **Soaring**, **Strong**, **Stumbling**, **Struggling**, and **Spiritless**.

It makes the case ideal congregations are **Soaring**. These congregations are effectively moving beyond ordinary ministry toward extraordinary ministry in a quest to achieve exceptional ministry in response to the pulling of God. They journey to places of inspiration, imagination, and innovation.

Soaring congregations are amazing Christ-centered communities of faith focused on Kingdom growth. Less than ten percent of all congregations are **Soaring**.

Great ministry is also provided by **Strong** congregations. **Strong** congregations add significant value to Christian ministry but are missing some essential characteristics that could morph them into **Soaring** congregations. This book identifies these missing traits.

Many **Strong** congregations are larger than the average congregation, and have outstanding programs, ministries, and activities. Slightly more than ten percent of all congregations fall into the **Strong** category.

The other 80 percent of congregations are **Stumbling**, **Struggling**, and **Spiritless**. They are composed of wonderful people created in God's image. They are often doing some meaningful things in Christian ministry. Yet, their congregation may be stuck, plateaued, declining, or even dying. Discontinuous, disruptive, or destructive intervention is required if they are ever to soar with faith.

Every congregation must assess and accept which collective best describes who they are right now. They need outside assistance to do this assessment. This establishes their beginning point for next steps. When they understand where they are, they can move forward on a spiritual and strategic journey.

This book helps *Soaring* congregations continue soaring. It points *Strong* congregations to the missing traits that could morph them into *Soaring* congregations.

Stumbling, *Struggling*, and *Spiritless* congregations learn about their situation and the need to begin a new kind of journey that could in five to seven years empower them to serve as *Strong* or *Soaring* congregations.

Read This Last at the end of this book explains how to connect with *The Greenville Hub: A Gathering to Dialogue About FaithSoaring Congregations* where you can come to South Carolina to learn how to assess your situation, along with what steps to take to launch an empowering spiritual and strategic journey.

On the next two pages is a chart that illustrates the *Soaring with Faith Congregations Typology*. This will give you an initial understanding of the typology. But be careful. At first glance you may declare you know which typology collective best describes your congregation.

What if you are wrong? I urge you not to make a shallow declaration. The future ministry of your congregation is more important than this. Every congregation must know where they are currently before they start taking—or fail to take—their next steps in Christian ministry.

My experience with this typology over the past three decades is that too many congregations who are *Strong* believe they are *Soaring*.

Soaring is a higher bar than many leaders truly grasp. *Soaring* is also a difficult focus to maintain more than five to seven years—once attained.

Stumbling congregations believe a turnaround for them is just around the next corner. They will be *Strong* once more. What they are experiencing now is only temporary. My experience tells me more than half of *Stumbling* congregations will next become *Struggling* congregations unless they address key issues quickly.

Finally, *Struggling* and *Spiritless* congregations underestimate the depth of transition and change needed to turn around. It could be more than they have time, energy, and resources to address.

What it all means is that knowing your starting point is a crucial first step and understanding the full typology is essential for knowing your starting point.

Soaring with Faith Congregations Typology

Missional Vitality	Percent of Whole	Description
Soaring	10% or less	A **Soaring** congregation has exceptional clarity and alignment regarding its mission, purpose, and core values. It is captured by God's empowering vision for its full potential focused on Kingdom growth. Clearly present are extraordinary vitality and vibrancy, leadership competency and trust, an external local and global missional focus, an effective disciple-making process, and creative ministry innovation.
Strong	15% or less	A **Strong** congregation has good clarity about its mission, purpose, core values, and vision. It has excellent programs, ministries, and activities intensely focused on discipleship development and active church membership. It pursues increased church growth through strategic plans it continually updates. Its missional engagement and creative ministry innovations are significant in their impact.
Stumbling	15-25%	A **Stumbling** congregation needs clarity about its mission, purpose, core values, and vision. Management of programs, ministries, activities, plus financial and facilities resources are their focus. The leadership wants a short-term fix but not a long-term solution. They need a spiritual and strategic journey but do not have the necessary readiness for change. They lack the capacity to be strong or soaring yet wish they could achieve it.

Struggling	25-30%	A *Struggling* congregation is smothered by their overly churched culture with an internal focus on making tomorrow a return of yesterday. The direct, dramatic, divine intervention of God is their faithful hope. They struggle to keep their programs, ministries, and activities functioning at a vital and vibrant level. The core of the congregation are often empty nesters and senior adults. They want to know what to do next year rather than taking a long look at their situation.
Spiritless	25-30%	A *Spiritless* congregation is a remnant group who are so culturally bound they cannot see the new thing God might do through them. The remnant is codependent on their congregational friends, rituals, and facilities. Their goal is to survive one more year. Without a radical new launch or planting they will one day cease to exist. They are fragile. They need the services of a trauma chaplain until there is an open door to confront them with the reality of their situation and the tough choices they must make.

Note: Copyright 2025 by George W. Bullard Jr. This typology is based on material originally developed by George Bullard.
It has been used and refined by others with whom George has collaborated. Among these are Chris Reinolds, Dave Rhodes, and Shane Stacey.

Introduction

A decade ago, I imagined I would be retiring within a few years. To prepare, I entered a ministry legacy season. During this time, I invited people to spend three days in my home for mentoring sessions—six people at a time—filled with active dialogue and great food prepared by my wife.

The focus was to share what I had learned about congregations, as well as the denominations and parachurch organizations that serve them, during five decades of research, writing, consulting, and coaching with congregations in more than 50 denominations.

I intended to pass on a legacy rather than just letting it fade away. I also wanted to keep learning from the people with whom I had these dialogues. Learning throughout life should never end.

My wife and I envisioned doing three of these per year for a season. They became so popular I led fifteen dialogues over the next four years: six in our home, two in other locations in Columbia, South Carolina, where we lived, and the others at various locations throughout North America.

The second part of my vision was to refocus on writing additional books that would create a lasting legacy in written form. However, that focus only resulted in one book instead of the seven I projected.

I did not retire when I thought I would. God had other plans. I was pursued and accepted a call for a five-year term as the director of an association of 100 Baptist congregations in the Midlands of South Carolina.

Then I retired.

Even then, I spent almost three years trying to learn how to say "No" to requests for consulting and mentoring services.

I am finally working on the second part: writing books. This is the first in a series I hope to write as my energy, ministry calling, and life learning enables.

The Focus of *Soaring with Faith*

This book presents a five set collective of congregations—*Soaring*, *Strong*, *Stumbling*, *Struggling*, and *Spiritless*. Every congregation can identify with one of these collectives more than the others. However, five to seven years ago they might have identified more with a different collective. Five to seven years from now, they might best identify with yet another collective.

This is because congregations are living organisms rather than static organizations. They are always in motion, transitioning, shifting, changing, and even morphing into different forms.

A minority of congregations are *Soaring* or *Strong*. Most congregations are *Stumbling*, *Struggling*, and *Spiritless* because they are not fully captured by God's vision for them. They desire what they want rather than what God wants. It depends on the factors influencing their missional vitality and vibrancy at any given season of their spiritual and strategic journey.

Categorizing congregations is a subjective assessment. Although supported by evidence and experience, it remains primarily intuitive for a third party like me. You need to determine for yourself where your congregation is in the collectives.

The Goal of this Focus

My goal is to help you understand where your congregation fits into these collectives of congregations and what it will require to move forward and even to soar with faith.

In doing this, I refer to my style as *Lyle Schaller Wisdom*, which I will explain shortly. Ministry colleagues close to me call my proclamations *Bullard-isms*. I'm fine with that.

The ideal is that every congregation is **Soaring**. The reality is that less than ten percent of all congregations are soaring with faith at any given time.

This book declares the ideal. My hope is for all congregations to aspire to soar with faith. Unfortunately, they do not. However, they can benefit from an understanding of their current situation. They can learn from the factors they must consider if they ever choose to fully surrender to God's mission and vision for them.

Congregations typically want to achieve success. Some desire to have a significant impact through their ministry. Few are willing to completely surrender to God's mission and vision for them. Those who are willing to fully surrender to God have the potential to soar with faith.

In this introduction, I am not defining what I mean by soaring with faith. Chapters one and two will provide that definition. Chapters three through seven will illustrate where it is found or absent throughout congregational collectives. Chapter eight will discuss various aspects of helping congregations soar with faith.

One important history about the collectives is that I first developed them in the mid-1990s, using the titles Perfecting, Pursuing, Preparing, Providing, and Presiding.

In the late 2010s, I made these collective titles available to those ministering through the former Future Church Company. They incorporated these collectives into their *Denominee* process where they taught denominational organizations and networks to differentiate how they served congregations on the basis of the collectives.

A successor group—Clarity House—also employs a

variation of these collectives in their ministry. Check them out at www.ClarityHouse.us.

The Mentoring Group

The storyline woven throughout this book revolves around a mentoring group meeting in my home. Here is an introduction to the group you will discover throughout the book. Each speaker is inspired by a specific participant in the mentoring experiences in my home and elsewhere but also represents a composite of various others present in different mentoring experiences. The individuals highlighted in this book came from six denominations, five states, and two countries.

- Becky is a retired laywoman from a mainline Protestant congregation who served as the chairperson for a spiritual and strategic journey process I led in her congregation. She attended to continue learning how to empower her congregation to soar with faith.
- Chad is a regional evangelical denominational leader, and a catalyst for church planting within his denomination and beyond. He is nationally known and highly regarded. Although we had never met before, we were aware of one another and had read things that each of us had written.
- Roger is a Protestant pastor in an affluent, high-density urban area who is seeking ways to adapt his ministry amid constant change. Although we had only met once or twice, we were very knowledgeable of each other through mutual friends and by our reputations.
- Melissa is a Christian journalist who writes articles about congregations and denominations across a broad spectrum of Christianity. We have known each

other for more than 30 years. Our ministries intersect regularly. She helped me with a book I wrote several years ago.

- Stewart is the national leader for an African American denomination. We previously served together in various ecumenical settings. I visited with him in his congregation several years ago. He has shown particular interest in my writings on denominations. He loves my phrase—*Real Denominations Serve Congregations*.
- Thomas is a pastor of a multisite congregation and a national leader for church planting in his small evangelical denomination. I worked with his denomination over several years in a consulting role focused on congregations that were soaring with faith. He wants to understand how to inspire ministry in various types of congregations, and particularly how to inspire them to launch new congregations and campuses.

The Congregational Case Studies

This book features case studies of congregations representing the collectives. Similar to the individuals participating in the mentoring experience, these case studies are fusions of various congregations encountered throughout a lifetime of ministry.

I was a consultant at some point with most of the case studies. Others I learned about from pastors and other ministry colleagues who told me their stories. I sought to present case studies that fit the collective where I share them.

Lyle Schaller Wisdom and Bullard-isms

Lyle E. Schaller—the leading consultant for congregations and denominations, a prognosticator, and a contrarian of the latter half of the 20th century in North America—was a key mentor for my consulting and writing ministry over a period of five decades. Therefore, it is important for me to talk about him in this book.

I began reading his writings in the late 1960s while in college. I first corresponded with him in the mid-1970s as part of a research project. Then I began training with him in the late 1970s. Over the next four decades, I had face-to-face interactions with him every few years. I was privileged to have him in my home on two occasions.

I was one of three people to whom he dedicated his 1995 book, *The New Reformation: Tomorrow Arrived Yesterday.*

Lyle informally mentored me and my ministry colleague and friend, Jere Allen, as we developed, launched, and expanded a national strategy for Baptists to assist congregations in transitional communities. Occasionally, he would share observations about our process. One that still resonates with me is when he said, "Too much data gets in the way of good decision-making."

He admonished us to experience congregations. Feel them. Touch them. Understand their spiritual passion or lack thereof. When necessary, gather hard data about them.

What he meant is that the heavy data-gathering process we used in the early years led us to determine our conclusions from the data. We used an overly left-brained approach. What we needed was to engage more deeply with the congregation and its people. That would bring out more right-brained impressions and insights which could enhance hard data.

We should draw conclusions and make recommendations consistent with the data but not constrained by it. We should allow our spiritual intuition and broad experience with many congregations to guide us in suggesting actions that would genuinely benefit the congregation.

What we knew, however, was that this must come from years of experience working with many different types of congregations. It took years to fully make the transition, but we did.

All of us—and even you the reader—may think we know congregations. But do we really feel and experience them as Lyle suggested?

Lyle discussed congregations and denominations in a consistent manner throughout his books, presentations, consulting, and mentoring. He shared intriguing societal and cultural data, along with research that underpinned many of his insights.

Lyle's personal life experiences enabled him to speak with authority and confidence on a wide range of topics within Christian ministry. Now, after nearly 50 years of consulting, coaching, researching, and writing about congregations and denominations, I get it.

In many areas of congregational and denominational ministry, I cannot explain how I know certain things. I just know them. I believe them. Some I developed myself or with ministry colleagues. I express them. I write them down. I recommend them. I evaluate congregations and denominations based on them.

I am also careful. I try to say, "In my personal experience the truth in this situation is …" This is the assurance of real experiences. Like Lyle, when convinced of new information and knowledge, my wisdom-sharing shifts. I am always learning.

What does this mean? In this book, you're not getting a dry, research-based, left-brained academic textbook. You're getting George Bullard. Or, as I mentioned earlier, you're getting *Bullard-isms*: my life convictions and biases combined.

Throughout the book, I try to be careful. Not reckless. I only share what I know or have experienced. I envision the future as I see it and share that perspective.

One example of being careful is the use of the word "most." I am still haunted by my college history adviser, David Knisley, who always warned against using the word "most" in any history paper unless I had taken a survey or could otherwise prove it. Since then, every time I read the word "most" in someone's writing, I question what they are saying.

If you see me use the word "most," please know that I have agonized over it.

My hope for you is that you move forward with high expectations for what you are about to read. I encourage you to seek clarification, push back, and engage in dialogue. May your ministry be blessed. May the congregations with whom you minister soar with faith.

– 1 –

Soaring with Faith Requires True Believers

It has been a great and fulfilling ministry life—thus far—as I look forward to what is next. My hope is for the breadth and depth of my experience to benefit the ministry of all readers of this material.

I choose to share who I am, my heritage, and a foundation for this book in this chapter. Now that I am in my mid-70s writing in the legacy season of my ministry, not as many people know of my ministry as knew about it in earlier years. My sole purpose in this chapter is for you to get to know me and any fleeting authority I have that allows me to speak on the subjects presented in this book.

My first paid congregational staff position was to direct music and youth at age 18. I planted my first congregation at age 19, became an associate pastor at 21, a pastor at 23 and was hired as a national consultant to congregations in transitional communities at age 26. Fifty years later, I am still mentoring congregations and pastors from time to time.

I grew up in a pastor's home and was well aware of the utter exhaustion that comes with congregational ministry. When I was in my mid-teens, my family moved to Philadelphia to launch new congregations in southeast Pennsylvania and southern New Jersey. From the very first day of our new ministry, I took an active role alongside my parents.

It marked the first phase of my joyous response to God's

call to Christian service. I felt and publicly declared my call to Christian ministry several years earlier in the congregation where my father served as pastor in Baltimore.

Over the next five decades, I worked as a staff member or pastor of congregations in three states; extensively researched and published findings on the responses of 100 congregations across 15 cities to demographic changes in their contexts over a period of 25 years; developed strategies for church planting, revitalization, and contextual ministry in 50 metropolitan areas of more than one million in population throughout the U.S.; consulted with congregations and movements in more than 50 denominations across North America; and led a denominational district of nearly 100 congregations for five years before my retirement.

I continue to search for strategies and characteristics that empower congregations to be much more than average. Ones that empower congregations to soar with faith beyond what seems possible or can be seen with human eyes. The faith-filled soaring I long to see requires our full heart, soul, mind, and strength, alongside spiritually imaginative ministry experience.

The longing to witness congregations soaring with faith beyond the ordinary patterns of the majority of congregations is something God inspired in me. However, I also say the lessons I learned at the breakfast, lunch, and supper table from my father instilled in me an appreciation for excellence in congregational life.

My father wanted to see congregations and their disciples soar with faith. He pushed so hard—too hard—to make it happen that it almost killed him. Two stomach ulcers and what was called a *nervous breakdown* in the middle of a sermon when I was 14 years old evidenced his attempt to strive for congregational excellence beyond what was humanly possible. It was and is only spiritually possible.

Dad came to understand this. It was just hard to accept this reality. His recovery from the emotional health crisis propelled him into the most significant years of his ministry. He shifted from pushing congregations to pulling them.

My father, like legions of pastors, sought during the majority of his ministry to push congregations he served to soar with faith. That cannot happen. Congregations must be pulled and guided forward by God's leadership to soar with faith to new heights.

Both God's inspiration and my father's example instilled in me a desire for congregations to fulfill their full Kingdom potential in the context where God leads them. Throughout my years in ministry, I sought to develop, write about, and lead processes that empower congregations to achieve their full Kingdom potential. My aim is not for them to grow large, but to be the best congregation they can be within their context, focusing on the people God has called them to serve.

Yet I always knew that no process designed by me or anyone else would enable them to soar with faith. Soaring goes beyond smart strategies into the realm of God's clear and empowering spiritual leading.

Congregations need help to soar. They cannot realize their full Kingdom potential without a willingness to lean into the direction that their spiritual discernment indicates God is guiding them, and to let God unfold it before them.

It Takes True Believers to Soar with Faith

One motivating memory of my first year in college is lying on the top bunk in my room, reading the book *The True Believer: Thoughts on the Nature of Mass Movements* by Eric Hoffer *(published by Harper & Row of New York in 1951)*. It was required reading for a long-forgotten introductory course. A controversial book and one that reveals the good, bad, and ugly of mass movements—those who start them, lead them, join them, follow them, and are changed by them.

It is a book about radicals involved in political, social, or religious mass movements. Religious mass movements continue to capture my attention today. The impact of this book was so significant that I find myself reading it again from time to time. With each new reading, I discover once more that mass movements can be used for both good and evil. Only a thin line separates these opposites.

During my first reading as a college freshman, I realized that a Christian mass movement centered on the unconditional love of God not only seemed natural but also represented the highest commitment for my life.

The message of Hoffer's book clarified and deepened my commitment to the ideal of a life-giving mass movement as a follower of Jesus. It helped me answer the question, "Is it worth giving my life?"

What can a journey of great faith—not just good faith—contribute to the eternal implications for all people? What is the best way to express great Christ-like faith?

My answer: It is the mass movement of exceptional Christian congregations who soar with faith beyond what is seen to what is unseen. It consists of communities of believers radically motivated by God's unconditional love to transform His world with spiritual ideals. They seek not to remake the world in their image, but to empower a world remade in God's image.

The True Believer is not a theological book, yet it declares and implies theology. Eric Hoffer was not a trained theologian, but he often speaks theologically throughout this work. It certainly affected my belief system and the actions of my life.

In my view, no other mass movement is as fitting as a full commitment to the Great Commission in the spirit of the Great Commandment. No other vehicle can better carry this mass movement than millions of Christian congregations worldwide simultaneously dedicated to gathering and scattering as God's radicals.

For me, this has meant a lifetime of high expectations for congregations that aspire to reach their full Kingdom potential. Congregations that are radical in their faith, utilizing methods that are loving not arrogant. Focused on sacrificial servanthood instead of confrontational hubris. Captivated by God's vision for how their congregation can fulfill His mission.

One result of my lifelong journey as a radical within the mass movement of Christianity is this book. In it I focus beyond congregations that are adequate, good enough, or even successful. The call of this book is for congregations to willingly soar with faith beyond any moniker researchers, prognosticators, denominations, or church growth and church health advocates choose to assign them.

The challenge is that a mass movement of soaring with faith congregations is unlikely due to the current commitment to mediocrity in the North American denomination and network scene. This mediocrity upholds the beaten path of cultural captivity. However, if the radical nature of the Christian message empowers a global mass movement that is sustainable, it could change this trend. Such a mass movement requires a multiplication of compassionate radicals beyond anything seen since Christianity's early decades.

In *The True Believer*, Eric Hoffer suggests these radicals exist. However, not all radicals are helpful and hopeful in a way that reflects the unconditional love of God. Some seek to control you, invade your country, psychologically abuse you, claim you as their own, and reshape you in their image instead of God's image.

Some of these negative radicals even lead congregations.

May all your passion focus on mass movements dedicated to the Good News of Jesus. Mine does. I am captivated by a positive, spiritual passion for the future to which God is leading us.

The Difference Maker

This book helps your congregation understand how to soar with faith beyond what you believe is your full Kingdom potential. The key takeaway is that soaring with faith is the difference maker for congregations. My hope is for your congregation to embrace and apply the principles and practices that make soaring possible within your unique context.

Commit today to be part of a soaring with faith movement.

It is insufficient to be growing, healthy, faithful, successful, revitalizing, innovative, flourishing, thriving, or to use any of the other popular terms employed to describe the successful to significant journey of congregations. This is particularly true because the Kingdom potential of congregations is far greater.

Soaring with faith is about full surrender to God's leading.

It is about soaring with faith beyond any benchmarks that a cacophony of screeching statistical measurements can produce. It is an "all in" surrender to the leadership of God's Holy Spirit that involves reaching the end of all artificially produced light and stepping into the darkness where only God's leadership lights the way.

The words defined in chapter two—*Soaring, Strong, Stumbling, Struggling, Spiritless*—are the five collectives of congregations. At any given time, every congregation falls into one of these categories. Congregations shift among these classifications throughout their lifespan.

Many congregations fail to soar with faith. They remain mediocre and are merely part of the great multitude of congregations.

Congregations might claim they are soaring simply because they have checked off specific metrics or finished a program on soaring congregations. However, that does not truly indicate soaring.

Even when people from a specific congregation claim they

are soaring, this may not actually be the case. They often self-declare without sufficient evidence to support their claims.

Other congregations strive to soar throughout their lives and are periodically successful in doing so. Soaring with faith requires guiding a congregation forward through God's empowering vision and continually journeying toward the goal of God's full Kingdom potential.

Soaring with faith isn't about finding one right way to do things. It's about discovering how God is working in and through your congregation, which empowers you to soar with faith. It's complex and even elusive. Instead of just one right way to soar, this book affirms 400,000 or more ways to soar. This represents the approximate number of Christian congregations throughout North America.

Every congregation has a unique spiritual calling for its life and ministry. They must either embrace that calling or reject it.

If you are seeking easy answers that have worked for dozens, hundreds, or thousands of other congregations, please stop reading now. You will be disappointed. Every congregation must discern and experience its unique calling from God.

What is God's call for your congregation? Do you know? Have you fully empowered it? Do you understand what it means to soar with faith?

I hope you understand soaring with faith by the end of this book. If God is calling your congregation to soar, I pray you hear and accept that call.

My Learning Background

"If building your congregation is all about you, then you don't need to worry about succession planning."

This was a provocative statement made years ago by management guru Jim Collins. In the mid-1990s, Collins addressed a gathering of pastors from the largest congregations in North America, discussing succession planning.

He told them if building their mega congregations was solely about themselves and what they could achieve, then they should not worry about succession planning. However, if building these congregations was about serving God, then they ought to spend 20 years engaging in succession planning.

I was one of the few people in that room who was not a lead pastor, but a congregational and denominational consultant. It was a transformative day hearing Collins—author of books such as *Built to Last, Good to Great, Great by Choice,* and *How the Mighty Fall*—discuss what it takes for a congregation to thrive over the long term, build the capacity to soar with faith, and continue soaring through a season of leadership succession.

Not a practicing Christian, Collins struggled to understand the spiritual implications of his own presentation. However, he clearly grasped the strategic implications that resonated with his audience. When I returned home, I collaborated with my team to reconceptualize the frameworks and tools we used in ways that provided clear pathways and core Christian principles.

I am still learning and receiving help from that day, along with other days when I had the privilege to learn at events sponsored by my friends at the Leadership Network of Dallas, Texas. In addition to what I learned from Collins, I also gained at these events insights from Peter Drucker—the father of modern management—which focused on the distinctions between the typical congregation, congregations striving to thrive, and the congregation evidently soaring with faith.

One influencer not nearly as well-known was Everett Rogers, author of *The Diffusion of Innovation.* He provided me with an understanding of the innovation curve that highlights the power of innovators and early adopters to ignite and create sustainable change in various life systems.

Adding Malcolm Gladwell's book, *The Tipping Point,* to

these encounters served as a clear catalyst for decades of congregational and denominational research, consulting, and writing that have led to this book.

This brings me to two personal learnings I want to share with you.

The First Learning

A key insight is to recognize that more than 90 percent of all congregations are not soaring with faith. Some never soar. Some soar for a while and then fall from the sky. Few soar for most of their lives. Others never grasp what it means to soar.

Congregational, denominational, and parachurch leaders undermine the essence of soaring with faith by implying that all congregations can soar, are soaring, or that every congregation can progress in the same manner by following a suggested strategy.

This represents a great disservice to congregations and God's Kingdom, resulting in tens of thousands of mediocre, plateaued, declining, culturally bound congregations. The less than ten percent of all congregations who are soaring with faith represent a benchmark of best practices that can inspire, motivate, and mentor other congregations.

The best way to advance a network of congregations is to assist those soaring with faith to regularly take a fresh look at their journey, and then to mentor potential soaring congregations. This will drive the entire network forward toward a greater experience of faith. While not all will soar, they will journey closer to their full Kingdom potential.

It helps strong congregations soar with faith, which creates the possibility for non-soaring congregations to respond to the inspiration, motivation, and mentoring from those who have discovered the narrow road forward to soaring.

Never say all congregations are or can soar. This is not true. It has a negative impact on a network of congregations by turning excellence into mediocrity. It creates a hopefulness that is mere fantasy. The idea of all congregations soaring is an unreachable ideal. It has never been and is unlikely to ever become a reality.

Consider these ideas about what occurs if soaring is deemed characteristic of all congregations:

- If all congregations are soaring, then no congregations are truly soaring.
- If all congregations are soaring, then the concept of soaring is meaningless.
- If all congregations are soaring, then there is no motivation to be better.
- If all congregations are soaring, then no congregations seek to stretch toward reaching their full Kingdom potential.
- If all congregations are soaring, then there is only one right way to engage in congregational life.
- If all congregations are soaring, then there is only one definition for soaring.
- If all congregations are soaring, then seldom are the variety of spiritual gifts acknowledged and affirmed.
- If all congregations are soaring, then there is no consideration for a diversity of various community contexts and affinity groupings.
- If all congregations are soaring, then all size congregations soar in the same way.

The Second Learning

Expressing the idea of soaring with faith is not straightforward. It isn't a measurable test given to a congregation. Rather, it is a subjective spiritual and strategic journey recognized over time.

It is not an assessment tool or exercise administered through before-and-after tests to show progress. Through left-brained assessment tools, progress occurs in parts of a congregation that do not affect the whole spiritual strategic journey of the congregation. Soaring with faith is a right-brained experience in community with others.

It is not like a congregational health checklist crafted by a self-declared expert which makes a soaring congregation. It is not a defined process. It is a Christ-centered experience.

Years ago, Lyle Schaller and I partnered to present at a conference. Our goal was to train a group of leaders from a missions education, support, and action organization that worked through congregations to build spiritual, leadership, and financial efforts for global missions. They sought to learn how to support congregations who were continually thriving and to ensure those congregations provided long-term backing for global missions.

A participant asked Lyle what he thought about the various congregational health inventories which were popular at that time. For what seemed like a long time, but was actually less than 30 seconds, Lyle rubbed his chin and gazed into the distance. Knowing Lyle well, I understood several things. He had an answer to the question. It was not going to be positive. He did not want to say it.

Then he looked at me and asked what I thought. I wasn't afraid to answer, so I said I do not like congregational health inventories because they are content-heavy and not process-oriented. They focus congregations on the image of the author of the inventory rather than on the image of God.

I suggested a more helpful inventory would identify critical issues congregations need to address to be healthy, or to become strong congregations with the potential to soar with faith. I then suggested spiritual discernment and in-depth dialogue within a congregation could lead to an understanding of where they are currently and where they need to be in order to soar with faith.

Lyle pointed at me and said, "That's it." The participants laughed.

Congregations can soar with faith only if they first address an understanding of God's leadership and certain key characteristics within their ministry context. These empowering characteristics may propel them to a position where both insiders and outsiders to the congregation affirm they are a congregation soaring with faith.

Soaring is discerned rather than mathematically determined. It is deeply experienced instead of communicated as a shallow, pithy statement or motto. It represents the pull of God rather than the push of humankind.

It is not determined by adherence to a denominational or network standard of performance, statistics in an annual report, or by the statement of the lead pastor or a lay leadership group. At best, these may indicate symptoms of short-term gain, rather than the establishment of a new congregational culture that is thriving in a sustainable manner.

Why Soaring with Faith Matters

Helping congregations soar with faith is personal to me. It reflects my response to God's call on my life. I am a firm believer in congregations who soar with faith. It is my destiny and passion. This is what I have dedicated my life to fulfill.

My commitment is radical. It is not about having successful or significant congregations. It is about having congregations fully surrendered to soaring with faith as the pathway to reach their full Kingdom potential.

I am captivated by God's vision for congregations. I have a positive, spiritual passion for the call of God for congregations to fulfill the Great Commission in the spirit of the Great Commandment.

Soaring with faith is essential for congregations. Each is called to realize God's full Kingdom potential for them, not just to be faithful, although that is foundational. Congregations must also be effective and innovative.

Earlier in this chapter, I contrasted the words "push" and "pull" regarding the movement of congregations. Many approaches to the future life and ministry of congregations focus on how they need to push forward to live into God's plan for them.

Too many pastors, staff, and lay leaders are *congregational pushers* promoting a programmatic or event drug too many people are buying. Congregations become addicted to this programmatic drug as they pursue temporal success instead of eternal significance and surrender to God's leading. In the long term, this has turned them into a *churched culture enclave* rather than a vital and vibrant missional community.

Too few pastors, staff, and lay leaders allow God to lead their congregations forward through the power of God's Holy Spirit. God's Spirit has already gone before them and seeks to show them the way.

The Holy Spirit goes before God-led congregations like a cloud by day and a fire by night. These congregations are soaring with faith toward the fulfillment of their full Kingdom potential. They have discarded the programmatic drug that causes them to **Stumble, Struggle**, and even feel **Spiritless**.

They have done everything they can to become **Strong**

congregations. Now they joyfully accept the pulling of God's Holy Spirit and are **Soaring**.

Soaring with faith is of extreme importance to the Kingdom of God. Let's move on to chapter two and discuss what it means to soar with faith.

SPIRITLESS

SOARING

– 2 –

What It Means
to Soar with Faith

"**D**uring this session, I will share that soaring with faith is an exceptional, ongoing journey of Christian ministry rather than a destination. To soar with faith means to be 'all in' from a Kingdom perspective."

Roger interrupted. "Wait a minute, George. You've been teasing us with what it means to soar with faith. Can you be more forthcoming? Can you clearly illustrate the concept for us?"

"Absolutely. I am sorry for the wait. I want to be sure you understand the significance of this approach to characterizing congregations. I am intentionally building a conceptual foundation. Soaring with faith is a complex issue that must be experienced rather than declared. I promise during this session we will focus on what it means to soar with faith."

"To illustrate soaring with faith, let me start with a story."

Soaring with Faith or Falling?

Karl Wallenda, the patriarch of The Flying Wallendas high-wire circus act, fell 75 feet to his death on March 22, 1978, while walking a cable strung between the two towers of the ten-story Condado Plaza Hotel in San Juan, Puerto Rico.

Reflecting on his death, his widow confirmed that during the months preceding the fall, Karl transitioned from an attitude of confidence and courage to one of fear and failure. He morphed from an aerialist who lived to soar into a hesitant high-wire actor consumed by the fear of falling.

This fear of falling is now known as The Wallenda Factor. It refers to situations where the fear of failure smothers the joy of success, significance, and surrender. It refers to situations where problem-solving erases *affirm-what's-right-and-build-on-it* processes, where counting the "no" votes is more important than counting the "yes" votes, and where emphasis is placed on things wrong rather than positive solutions.

Too many congregations struggle to soar with faith because they fear falling more than they are inspired to walk by faith. They are more afraid of failure than they are exhilarated by rejoicing.

They concentrate their thinking on fixes rather than solutions, focusing on the short-term rather than the long-term. They prioritize boxed sets over centered sets. They propel themselves forward through their own efforts instead of letting God lead them forward. They do not soar—whether or not they have faith.

The Wallenda Factor expresses itself in congregations when a threat is present. People fear this threat will become a reality and harm will come to their congregation.

Dialogue often centers on the possibility of something negative happening to the congregation rather than the prospect of soaring with faith.

I often ask, "Is your congregation soaring with faith? If so, what is the evidence? Or is your congregation falling, failing, or simply too commonplace?"

My prayer for your congregation is for you to walk by faith rather than by sight in the spirit of 2 Corinthians 5:7. It's what we trust in but don't yet see that keeps us going.

Selected Reflections from the Mentoring Group

"That is a nice inspirational story and concept about the feeling and commitment to soaring with faith, but we are not going to let you off that easy," said Melissa with a hint of demand in her voice. "What does it mean to soar with faith?"

"Well said, Melissa!" added Steward. "George, give us more."

"What I have is a handout," I responded. "I believe Melissa sneaked a peek at the title. Here it is."

What Does It Mean to Soar with Faith?

Imagine with me what it would be like for congregations to soar with faith.

Congregations who soar with faith exemplify exceptional ministry rather than ordinary ministry.

They boldly and effectively leap into a future known only to God, one they have never ventured into before and cannot see at the beginning of their journey. They willingly leave behind the past and move forward toward what lies ahead of them.

Congregations who effectively soar with faith reject ordinary ministry and embrace extraordinary ministry in a quest to achieve exceptional ministry. They respond to the pulling of our God who goes before them. Experiences of inspiration, imagination, and innovation fill their journey.

They progress through processes of missional formation and engagement that effectively connect the Good News with the people they serve. They continually transform their capacity to reach their full Kingdom potential.

Willingly, they go to the end of all known light or revelation, and leap into the darkness because they know God has gone before them. Leaps of faith and extraordinary commitments are the new normal for post-pandemic congregations soaring with faith. Boldly, they journey into the future as God reveals the pathway for their journey.

As my long-term colleague in ministry, Leonard Sweet, said, "To step forth in faith is by definition to step over the line." What lies beyond the line is known only by God and thus involves continual steps of faith by the traveler.

Selected Reflections from the Mentoring Group

"George," interrupted Thomas, "I need some biblical references to wrap my arms around this concept. What can you offer us?"

"Try two from the next handout as initial references. See if you can preach and teach on them," I suggested.

Biblical Illustrations of Soaring with Faith

Like Abram in Genesis 12, soaring with faith congregations gather their possessions and embark on a journey into the unknown due to their faith in God's leadership. Their faith empowers them to soar. While they may not see the future any clearer than other congregations, they do see with trusting eyes the One who knows the future and draws them toward it.

> GOD told Abram: "Leave your country, your family, and your father's home for a land that I will show you. I'll make you a great nation and bless you. I'll make you famous; you'll be a blessing. I'll bless those who bless you; those who curse you I'll curse. All the families of the Earth will be blessed through you." (Genesis 12:1–3)

Like the Israelites after the Exodus, their journey is guided by God, with a cloud by day and fire by night. These congregations clearly see and meaningfully discern the directional signs of God's influence on their ministry.

> They moved on from Succoth and then camped at Etham at the edge of the wilderness. GOD went ahead of them in a Pillar of Cloud during the day to guide them on the way, and at night in a Pillar of Fire to give them light; thus, they could travel both day and night. The Pillar of Cloud by day and the Pillar of Fire by night never left the people. (Exodus 13:21–22)

"This is just a reference piece," I said quickly before the group jumped on me again. "Let me show you in a handout several ideas and word patterns I have used over the years to differentiate a soaring with faith congregation from the typical congregation."

Words and Concepts Along the Journey of Congregations

During decades of consulting and coaching with congregations and denominations, I have used various words and concepts that inform my current understanding of soaring with faith. In some cases, one word or a single concept fit. In other cases, as in the first one, all three words or concepts are essential to understanding the richness of soaring with faith.

See which one or more of these connect with your feelings and thoughts about soaring with faith.

These terms inspire a journey of soaring with faith when applied with genuine ownership within congregations. No guarantee. Just realistic hope.

Faithful, Effective, and Innovative Congregations: Congregations who soar with faith are faithful, effective, and innovative. They are faithful to the core Gospel and the ethos of their denomination or network. They are effective in missional formation and engagement while pursuing excellence at every opportunity. They are innovative and ever changing in methodologies, always looking for new and relevant ways to tell the never changing story of Jesus.

All three are necessary for congregations to soar with faith. Let's take this idea farther.

First, regarding faithfulness, I suspect a majority of congregations in North America are merely embodying the life of a faithful congregation. Their focus is on the past, on memories, and on tradition as they seek to be faithful to God's guidance to them.

Their faithfulness to the Good News of Jesus and their traditions are supported at all costs. While this is positive in many respects, it can also be negative because effectiveness and innovation are not part of their journey.

Typically, when I hear a congregation claim their best characteristic is faithfulness, I immediately think the following: They are lagging. They aren't doing much. But at least they are faithful.

Second, some congregations are both faithful and effective. They focus on the present. In addition to their faithfulness, they have the capacity and vision to function with effectiveness. They connect well with their context only if that context does not radically and quickly change.

They may have a few best practices others emulate. However, they do not change when their congregation and their community transitions. They may drift into a pattern of hoping tomorrow will bring a return of yesterday because what they once did worked for them.

These congregations pursue church growth through an

emphasis on programs, ministries, and activities. They want people to commit to participation in growth events and projects, and for this approach to be effective.

Third, faithfulness, effectiveness, and innovation represent a worthy goal, yet a small percentage of congregations are characterized by all three. Those congregations characterized by all three are faithful to the Good News and to their traditions. They strive for effectiveness in everything they do and continuously evaluate the impact of their actions.

Innovation is a key principle that distinguishes them from many other congregations. They continuously innovate their methodologies to remain faithful to the Good News and ensure their disciplemaking effectiveness is relevant to the people to whom God is sending them for them to be received by those to whom they go.

If they soar with faith, it is because they address these three—faithfulness, effectiveness, and innovation—and focus on the emerging future where God has gone before them and shows the way. Pulling them forward.

These congregations pursue Kingdom growth—more than church growth—and want every Christian disciple to understand the call of God on their lives as they serve as the scattered Christian Church engaged in missional ministry.

Successful, Significant, and Surrender Congregations: This is a concept I learned through the life story of Bob Buford, founder of Leadership Network in Dallas, Texas. It highlighted the significance of the continuum of the words *success, significance,* and *surrender.* I often heard him share his story, which is recounted in his book *Halftime: Moving from Success to Significance.*

When I heard Bob talk about how his own life halftime experience led him to move from success in the cable television industry to doing something significant, it resonated with where I was in my life.

A key mentor for Bob during his halftime was the 20th-century management guru Peter Drucker. He helped Bob shift from a focus on success to one on significance. It was a pleasure to hear Drucker discuss this during the latter part of his life.

I later heard Bob say the renowned Catholic priest Henri Nouwen suggested to him he would begin to arrive at maturity in his life journey when he fully surrendered to God. I realized then I was shown a cosmic wormhole to a different place in the universe for helping congregations rapidly accelerate and soar with faith.

These three words embody congregations soaring with faith: success, significance, and surrender.

First, congregations can achieve success in their growth efforts, but organizational success alone is not enough. They must prioritize the eternal lives of people over the numbers they seek to acquire. They must focus on the growth of God's Kingdom rather than the expansion of humanity's congregational organizations.

Second, congregations must also address significant spiritual and strategic issues in a way that fosters deep transition and change, leading to ongoing transformation. Ultimately, congregations may fully surrender to God's leadership as the only guidance that will enable them to soar in faith. As a result, God's eternal mission and foresight propel them forward, rather than having them push ahead with their own limited, finite mission and vision.

Third, congregations who soar with faith have moved on beyond success and significance to full surrender to God. They accelerate through the cosmic wormhole to a whole new world of ministry. They are a great beauty to behold.

Perfecting Congregations: Thirty years ago, I worked on an early version of the current collectives of congregations. I referred to those soaring with faith as perfecting congregations.

Perfecting congregations are those already on a spiritual

and strategic journey to achieve their full Kingdom potential. They know who they are, what they value and believe, where they are headed, and how they will get there. They are simply continuously perfecting that journey. They possess clarity and alignment.

At the same time, they are not overconfident, nor are their leaders filled with hubris. They remain continually open to the new things God reveals to them along their journey. As they travel, they reach locations that provide a clearer perspective on their path.

In the spirit of the Last Battle in *The Chronicles of Narnia* by C. S. Lewis, they can see farther up and farther into the journey God has for them. You will never hear them say they have arrived at the end of their journey. Always, there is a next place where God is going before them and pulling them.

They stay focused on the goal described in Philippians 3:12–16.

"I'm not saying that I have this all together, that I have it made. But I am well on my way, reaching out for Christ, who has so wondrously reached out for me. Friends, don't get me wrong: By no means do I count myself an expert in all of this, but I've got my eye on the goal, where God is beckoning us onward—to Jesus. I'm off and running, and I'm not turning back.

"So let's keep focused on that goal, those of us who want everything God has for us. If any of you have something else in mind, something less than total commitment, God will clear your blurred vision—you'll see it yet! Now that we're on the right track, let's stay on it."

Vision Plus Intentionality: The research that launched my ministry as a congregational consultant 50 years ago was a multiple year project on 100 congregations in 15 metropolitan areas throughout the USA who were in transitional communities affected by change in multiple demographics. The five demographic changes were race, ethnicity, socioeconomics, lifestyle, and population density.

Many of these congregations were plateaued, declining, and dying. Nine had died within the ten-year period of the study. Another 22 had relocated, merged with other congregations, were adopted by another congregation, invited a congregation of another race or ethnicity to become the primary congregation in their facilities, or replanted themselves in the same location or another.

Only one-third were growing. The ultimate focus of the research sought to discover what empowered some to thrive—even to soar with faith—while others died. Was it the right strategy? Was it the right combination of programs? Was it finances? Was it leadership? Obviously, in these congregations one or more of these factors were present. But that was not the key factor discovered.

The key factor was the congregations who experienced growth in vitality and vibrancy possessed a clear understanding of God's empowering vision for them. They were inspired by a spiritual vision to soar with faith. Consequently, the congregational strategies and actions were intentionally aligned to fulfill this vision. Specific prescribed programs, ministries, and activities of the congregation were not a key factor.

The research took place during a time of great debate about whether the best strategy in diverse metropolitan areas was evangelism followed by ministry, or social ministry followed by evangelism. Neither was true. Congregations using both approaches were thriving. Clarity of vision plus intentional alignment of their programs, ministries, and activities to fulfill God's vision for them were the keys to flourishing in faith.

When presenting this research, I summarize the results in three words: *Vision Plus Intentionality*. Congregations soaring with faith possess *Vision Plus Intentionality*.

(Note to the Reader: You will see vision and intentionality reframed in this book as clarity and alignment.)

As challenging as it is for congregations to be captivated by God's empowering vision, it is even more challenging for them to commit to and sustain intentional strategies and actions that align with the vision. People often want to add programs and projects that do not fulfill the vision but better align with their past to present culture and traditions.

Congregations soaring with faith have permission-giving leaders who do two things.

First, they ensure the formal programs, ministries, and activities of the congregation, along with the deployment of staff and volunteers, focus on initiatives that will fulfill the vision.

Second, by utilizing a permission-giving process that empowers individuals to experiment with programs, ministries, and activities that may not seem to fit, leaders grant authority to try out new ideas without requiring the congregation to provide resources. If their idea succeeds, the congregation can then endorse these new initiatives and consider their approach in the next wave of innovation.

Selected Reflections from the Mentoring Dialogue

"George, this is a lot of different frameworks for identifying congregations who are soaring with faith," Becky pointed out. "The average layperson in a congregation is not going to get all that language. What can you do to simplify it?"

"That's a great question, Becky. In the constellation of Who, What, When, Where, Why, and How, here is the When followed by the What. See if this helps."

25

When are Congregations Soaring with Faith?

Congregations soar with faith when captivated by God's empowering vision, and then intentionally align all their ministries for the fulfillment of that vision. This can be summed up in three words: *Vision Plus Intentionality*, or, as we will discuss moving forward as *Clarity Plus Alignment*.

Congregations soar with faith when they embark on a positive, passionate, and purposeful spiritual and strategic journey with an extraordinary commitment to God to achieve, sustain, and continuously re-envision exceptional ministry that is Christ-centered, faith-based, and contextually relevant.

They embark on this journey because they have surrendered their ministry to God, who goes before them and pulls them into the contexts or people groups they are called to serve. The journey never ends. Congregations never declare they have arrived. They practice the discipline of sabbatical every seven years and jubilee every 50 years by following the pattern illustrated in Leviticus 25:1–12.

They are marked by an extraordinary commitment to clarity, alignment, people, faith, worship, expectations, connections, community, wellbeing, and generosity. These ten characteristics shape five congregational collectives.

What is the Meaning of Soaring with Faith?

The soaring with faith theme is not a specific or standardized term in North American Protestant Christianity. Its meaning may vary depending on the context and beliefs of the congregation using it. Nevertheless, soaring with faith suggests a convincing and unwavering belief in God's *Missio Dei* or the mission of God, and a deep trust in His guidance. It reflects an eagerness to follow His direction and how He pulls us forward to our full Kingdom potential.

It also indicates congregations may undergo a period of growth or renewal, with members feeling particularly inspired, uplifted, and connected to God. This could result from various factors, such as powerful worship services, insightful Bible study, meaningful fellowship that fosters a strong community, missional efforts, and personal experiences of spiritual awakening.

Ultimately, the exact meaning of soaring with faith depends on the specific beliefs and practices of the congregation in question, along with the personal experiences and perspectives of its members.

Congregational Collectives

A generation ago, when I began working on a typology for congregations based on their missional vitality, I spoke about it, trained denominations to use it, loaned it to team members of a national consulting group, and granted individuals permission to use it. But I never fully developed it in writing.

This typology describes the full spectrum of congregations, from those soaring with faith to those lacking a congregational-wide faith journey. Here is a brief overview of the five types of congregations, which I now refer to as congregational collectives.

The first collective focuses on congregations soaring with faith as that is the goal for all congregations. The other four talk about congregations who are not yet or perhaps once were soaring with faith.

The keywords for the five types of congregations are *Soaring*, *Strong*, *Stumbling*, *Struggling*, and *Spiritless*. The next five chapters will provide a more detailed characterization of each of these types.

Soaring: A *Soaring* congregation has exceptional clarity and alignment regarding its mission, purpose, and core values. It is captured by God's empowering vision for its full potential focused on Kingdom growth. Clearly present are extraordinary vitality and vibrancy, leadership competency and trust, an external local and global missional focus, an effective disciple-making process, and creative ministry innovation.

Strong: A *Strong* congregation has good clarity about its mission, purpose, core values, and vision. It has excellent programs, ministries, and activities intensely focused on discipleship development and active congregational membership. It pursues increased church growth through strategic plans it continually updates. Its missional engagement and creative ministry innovations are significant in their impact.

Stumbling: A *Stumbling* congregation needs clarity and alignment about its mission, purpose, core values, and vision. Management of programs, ministries, activities, plus financial and facilities resources are their focus. The leadership wants a short-term fix, but not a long-term solution. They need a spiritual and strategic journey but lack necessary readiness for change. They lack the capacity to be *Strong* or *Soaring*, but desire to achieve it.

Struggling: A *Struggling* congregation is smothered by their overly churched culture with an internal focus on making tomorrow a return of yesterday. The direct, dramatic, divine intervention of God is their faithful hope. They struggle to keep their programs, ministries, and activities alive. The core of the congregation are often empty nester and senior adult households. They want to know what to do next year rather than taking a long look at their situation.

Spiritless: A *Spiritless* congregation is a remnant group who are so culturally bound they cannot see the new thing

God might do through them. The remnant is codependent on their congregational friends, rituals, and facilities. Their goal is to survive one more year. Without a radical new launch or planting they will cease to exist. They are fragile. They need the services of a trauma chaplain until there is an open door to confront them with the reality of their situation and the tough choices they must make.

The Ten Characteristics of Soaring Congregations

In the next five chapters, I will also reference ten characteristics of soaring congregations and how they are expressed, or not expressed, in each collective.

Along the way, I suggest each needs to transform to soar with faith. How they can rise to the level of full surrender to God's leadership instead of merely remaining in the realm of success and potential significance.

The characteristics reflect a perspective based on what I believe I have learned over the past six decades about what it takes for congregations to soar with faith. However, they are dialogical—not declarative. I am not asserting that the ten characteristics as I articulate them must be the exact traits of congregations to soar with faith. They simply represent my current understanding.

I suggest these ten characteristics for congregations to engage in spiritual and strategic dialogue as they journey toward a place where they can soar with faith. I present these briefly from a soaring with faith perspective to establish the desired standard. A longer version is in Chapter Three.

1. **Clarity:** *Soaring* congregations have and continually freshen their clarity around their mission, purpose, core values, and vision.

29

2. **Alignment:** *Soaring* congregations radically align their programs, ministries, and activities with their clarity as they seek to achieve and maintain exceptional ministry.

3. **People:** *Soaring* congregations know in profound ways the people or community God is calling them to serve.

4. **Faith:** *Soaring* congregations involve people in faith formation through an ongoing disciplemaking journey.

5. **Worship:** *Soaring* congregations have inspiring, impactful worship experiences.

6. **Expectations:** *Soaring* congregations have high expectations of all members that they are living out God's call on their lives.

7. **Connections:** *Soaring* congregations seek to connect preChristians, unchurched, underchurched, and dechurched people with Jesus and their congregational family.

8. **Community:** *Soaring* congregations are places of great, in-depth community where people build deep relationships with one another.

9. **Wellbeing:** *Soaring* congregations have systems and structures that are healthy, avoid conflict, and build deep unity.

10. **Generosity:** *Soaring* congregations help members realize that all we have belongs to God and they should honor His mission with great sacrifice of talents, time, and finances.

Consider Your Congregation

With this foundation, begin thinking about where your congregation is in their faith journey. Is your congregation *Soaring, Strong, Stumbling, Struggling,* or *Spiritless*?

From this point forward in reading this book, you can either read the chapters in order or jump around to find the one that best describes your congregation.

If **Soaring**, are you clear on how you got there, how you will maintain a soaring journey, what it might look like if you lose your soaring nature, or what to do if you are no longer soaring?

If you are **Strong**, let me warn you now that you might try to convince me you are **Soaring**. I will probably push back because you may be missing some traits that keep you from being **Soaring**.

If you are **Stumbling**, **Struggling**, or **Spiritless**, what will it take for you to gain the spiritual and strategic capacity to soar with faith? Is it even possible for your congregation? I hope so, as we need more **Soaring** congregations.

Selected Reflections from the Mentoring Dialogue

Melissa, the Christian journalist in the group, said, "Soaring with faith is a complex concept to get in a 700-word news article. At the same time, the succinct statements do not provide enough detail to clearly explain the concepts."

I responded, "Yes, I believe understanding soaring with faith cannot happen in a 25- or less word statement or a 700-word news article. It is a complex or learned understanding. If it was easy more congregations would be soaring. It is hard to measure, but a thing of great beauty when a congregation gets it."

SOARING

- 3 -

Soaring Congregations Pursue Their Full Kingdom Potential

*A **Soaring** congregation has exceptional clarity and alignment regarding its mission, purpose, and core values. It is captured by God's empowering vision for its full potential focused on Kingdom growth. Clearly present are extraordinary vitality and vibrancy, leadership competency and trust, an external local and global missional focus, an effective disciplemaking process, and creative ministry innovation.*

Back to the mentoring session …

"As we begin this session on soaring congregations, I want to start with an illustration of a congregation who is soaring with faith. It is affiliated with Stewart's denomination, but I hear, Stewart, you did not know about this church," I said as I started the afternoon session following some great food and fellowship around our dining room table.

"That's right," Stewart offered. "Thank you for sharing this story with me when I responded to the invitation to be part of this dialogue. I am going to plan a trip to find out more about this great missionary story."

Life as a soaring congregation can be elusive. Far fewer congregations are truly soaring than the number who claim to be.

It requires the ability to sustain missional engagement in the context where God has sent you to be received.

Consider the congregation at Mount Calvary.

Mount Calvary Surrenders to God's Leadership for Their Community Context

"I am going to shoot those church people who come to my farm to pick up my workers and take them to English classes. I don't want these Mexicans learning English. They might try to stay here and become US citizens. I am sending them home when I am finished with them."

This was the warning Lillian Gaines received from one of the farmers in the county. It really scared her. As a black woman who had lived in this county all her life, she knew the farmer who sent that note was serious.

She and her pastor gathered their ministry leaders to share the message, then pray and decide what to do. They determined they could not stop the ministry to which God had called them.

Their decision was to continue and get word to the migrant workers to walk to the road outside all the farms as they would not be able to pick them up inside the farms anymore.

This worked. They never heard anything more from the farmers where they picked up migrants to go to English classes.

Who is Lillian Gaines? Lillian Gaines, a retired school-teacher who served as a reading specialist, was an active leader in the Mount Calvary congregation. This congregation is in the unincorporated community of Allen Crossroads. The population in this village is less than 500. Five congregations are in the area. Mount Calvary formed near the end of the Civil War when emancipated slaves came together as a new congregation.

All five Allen Crossroads congregations have between 35

and 55 in attendance. Almost everyone in the community claims membership in one of the congregations. Only five families claim no congregational membership. A popular story around the community is that every congregation has visited these families multiple times trying to "get them saved."

Lillian was no exception. In retirement she decided to befriend each of these families with the hope she might be able—with the Holy Spirit's help—to convince them to become followers of Jesus. In visiting these families, she discovered the parents in one household could not read and write above a third-grade level. Once she had gotten close to this family, she explained her professional ability to the parents and offered to help them with their literacy skills.

They accepted.

Over the next 18 months she worked weekly with the husband and wife and dramatically increased their reading level. She used a simplified version of the New Testament as parallel reading. Through this in-depth relationship, the parents began asking questions about what it meant to follow Jesus and accept Him as their Savior and Lord.

Lillian answered their questions and prayed with them. A group of women in Mount Calvary also prayed for them. Ultimately, the parents and all four children became baptized followers of Jesus at Mount Calvary.

Lillian had leadership skills and great passion for what she felt God would have her do. While tutoring these parents, she also organized a group of people in her congregation to be literacy tutors for other adults in their county. Her pastor and congregational elders blessed her ministry. Eventually she recruited other congregations in the village to help. Mount Calvary commissioned her as a missionary to Allen Crossroads and the surrounding areas.

Obviously in a congregation the size of Mount Calvary this became the major ministry beyond their regular worship services. Their pastor was covocational and drove from his home more than an hour away to preach on Sundays and for other pastoral duties.

Until Lillian's retirement, Mount Calvary was primarily a preaching station and community gathering place. Now it was coming alive as it saw people, their spiritual development, and missionary work in the community as their God-given focus. They were soaring with faith.

But this is not the end of the story. The need for literacy missions in the county was greater than Mount Calvary could handle. Their county was poor. Years ago, it dropped its focus on adult literacy when insufficient government funding was available.

Lillian and the Mount Calvary congregation determined they could take the lead in a community-based adult literacy program. Mount Calvary sponsored training for tutors. All five congregations helped discover people in need of and willing to accept tutoring.

What pleased Lillian and Mount Calvary was the spiritual nature of this ministry as people learned to care holistically about one another. The focus of the congregations historically was on the people already connected with their congregations. Now they saw people who were outside their congregations becoming their primary concern. Within two years more than 130 people received tutoring from almost 60 trained tutors.

The impact on all congregations was obvious. The community congregations began holding annual weekends where they would pray, rejoice, dialogue, and plan the next year of ministry. They became captured by God's empowering vision for their congregations. Yes, this was more than a short-term revival. They were soaring with faith and in anticipation of the next thing God would do in and through them to spiritually transform their community context.

Something Else was Next! During an annual missions weekend at Mount Calvary the idea of broadening their ministry arose when talking about immigrant farm workers in the area from Mexico and other Central American countries. The immigrants wanted to learn English and to go through the U.S. citizenship process. But just the idea alone caused controversy. What if they are illegals? Criminals? Does this take the focus off African Americans? What will the farm owners say about their workers learning English and U.S. laws?

Each of these concerns had legitimate points. After months of prayerful consideration and discussions with farmers and county officials, this new dimension of ministry began.

What about the immigrant farm workers? Would they respond during these troubling times? This became the least of concerns. More concerning was having enough tutors trained in English as a Second Language to respond to the multiple requests to take part in the classes. Coordination was complicated. When to conduct the classes that would not interfere with their work. How to supply transportation. Meals became an issue as the farm workers missed meals provided to them by the farmers.

Eventually there arose resistance from the farmers as the farm workers began to read and learn about American laws and their rights. One farmer—as noted above—even threatened violence—"shooting those church people"—if they continued to come on his farm to pick up workers. Ultimately even this was overcome.

Among the farm workers were a high percentage of people who were not Christians or were lapsed Catholics. As Christians tutored them, they began to learn more about being a follower of Jesus. Some became Christians or renewed a Christian commitment they had not practiced for years. The request then came for them to have a congregation composed of people from Central America.

The sponsoring congregations launched the new congregational expression by finding a pastor, a meeting place, furnishing it, providing essential supplies, and praying fervently for the effort. Allen Crossroads now had six congregations and it felt good.

The Rest of the Story: During this missional activity, what happened to Lillian Gaines and Mount Calvary that made them a congregation soaring with faith and focused more on community transformation and Kingdom growth rather than directly on church growth?

Through the initiatives that began with the inspiration of Lillian Gaines, Mount Calvary discovered the people God called them to serve. They did not at once have clarity and alignment. They arrived at it through an action then reflection approach. Following the initiation of one or two of the new ministries, they began a dialogue on what God's voice was saying to their congregation about vision clarity plus alignment.

They began to discern clarity and how to align everything with this clarity. This came after congregational prayer, powerful messages by their pastor, testimonies by laypersons involved in the ministries, specialized ministry training, and dialogue with the people God called them to serve.

Their pastor supplied the spiritual focus. But it was a group of women in the congregation who planned, promoted, and led in the practice of the God-inspired ministries. It also created a ministry partnership that crossed denominational lines, theological perspectives, and racial and ethnic barriers. It produced a community-wide and eventually a county-wide ministry focus.

The strength of what God created, revealed itself in an obvious way when health issues caused Lillian Gaines to no longer be able to lead the effort. Through her commitment, humility, and foresight a strong, broad, and multi-congregational leadership base emerged that carried on the ministry when the opportunity to lead was no longer hers.

Reflections from the Mentoring Group

I asked, "What is your response to this as a case study about congregations soaring with faith?"

"I am confused," Chad said while shaking his head. "I would assume a soaring congregation is one that is much larger. Perhaps even mega or multi-site."

Stewart jumped in. "Of course, I love it. It is one of my congregations. One of my pastors. A missionary woman filled with God's Spirit. Yet, it is unexpected by me also. I would have thought size mattered too."

"No, it is probably a good example," said Melissa. "Many congregations I write about are this size. Some of them have high quality ministries like this. I think it fits."

I can really identify with Lillian," said Becky, breathing heavy with a sense of burden. "I almost cried from the opening words about the farmer's threat. I love compassion ministry. I have been in situations not all that different from this. It is that call of God to ministry that pulls us forward that causes my heart to beat faster. If this is what soaring with faith is all about, I'm in."

"Thank you, Becky, and others for your response. Let me address the size issue," I said, transitioning the dialogue in this teachable moment.

Are Soaring Congregations Only Very Large, Mega, or Multi-Site Congregations?

Not necessarily. It does seem natural to think they would be. Many are. Many are not.

They might be smaller membership congregations with a weekly engagement of less than 100 people. It depends. Or they could be anywhere along the spectrum from small to mega. Size is not the point. The two most significant points are that they have clarity and alignment.

Clarity: *Soaring* congregations have and continually freshen their clarity around their mission, purpose, core values, and vision. They use timely hinge points in their spiritual and strategic journey to ask God to speak into their clarity and depth of ownership of their mission, purpose, values, and vision. God's empowering vision is always fresh and empowers congregations to soar farther in the direction where God is pulling them.

Alignment: *Soaring* congregations intentionally align their programs, ministries, and activities with their clarity as they seek to achieve and maintain exceptional ministry. They address alignment with great frequency. Not to change for change's sake, but to keep their actions in great alignment with their response to any freshening of their clarity.

Clarity plus alignment is essential for any congregation to attain the status of *Soaring*. Without a clear vision of where and how God is empowering a congregation along its journey, and an intentional commitment to and practice of aligning everything it does to fulfill God's vision, there is no soaring.

If the community context or the people group or groups they serve are of sufficient size, with a continual influx of new residents in new housing or housing that is turning over, then they may also grow to be larger than the typical congregation. Perhaps very large to mega in size. It all depends on the context they serve.

Mount Calvary and their partner congregations serve a rural and small-town county of no more than 30,000 people. The county experienced a 17-percent decline in their population over the past 30 years. That they are growing at all is amazing. In their context, they are the mega ministry congregation.

How Do Soaring Congregations Address the Other Characteristics?

People: *Soaring* congregations know in profound ways the people or community God is calling them to serve. They are sensitive to and act on transitions and changes in the demographic, lifestyle, and spiritual needs of the community context, or the people God is calling them to serve now and in the future. As they imagine their ministry, they begin their strategic conversation by talking about the people who need to receive God's unconditional love rather than the programs they want to launch.

Faith: *Soaring* congregations involve people in faith formation through an ongoing disciplemaking journey. They desire for more people to connect with them, but rather than just as members, their desire is for people who want to be on a lifelong faith formation and disciplemaking journey in response to God's call on their lives. Their heart desire is for people to become fully devoted followers of Christ.

Worship: *Soaring* congregations have inspiring, impactful worship experiences. They go beyond high quality or performance worship, to worship which helps people encounter God speaking into their lives. The people who attend worship reflect the encounter in their lives outside of worship as they are motivated toward missional engagement.

Expectations: *Soaring* congregations have high expectations of all members that they are living out God's call on their lives. They desire to eliminate mediocrity in favor of a high expectations community of people with positive spiritual passion about the movement of God in their lives and congregation. Mediocre ministry, or ministry for ministry sake, is shunned by these congregations.

Connections: *Soaring* congregations seek to connect preChristians, unchurched, underchurched, and dechurched people with Jesus and their congregational family. They are passionate about creating intentional and ongoing relationships for people to receive Jesus and know that faith formation requires ongoing nurturing for people to becoming fully devoted followers of Christ.

Community: *Soaring* congregations are places of great, in-depth community where people build deep relationships with one another. They build meaningful relationships and genuine community. They produce fewer congregation refugees who leave the practice of Christianity because of the depth of care for the spiritual, social, physical, and other life needs of people.

Wellbeing: *Soaring* congregations have systems and structures which are nourishing, address conflict proactively, and build enduring unity. They have integrative systems and structures that take great care to exhibit positive spiritual life as a living organism. They are sensitive to the dynamics of typical congregational life, and even the occasional conflict and trauma.

Generosity: *Soaring* congregations help members realize all they have belongs to God and they should honor His mission with great sacrifice of talents, time, and finances. They express generosity and a giving of time, talents, and tithes as a foundation for Christian living. Beyond this foundation is a call to go beyond success, significance, and achieve surrender to God with all that they are and have.

Here is another example of a *Soaring* congregation with a different context, size, and ministry.

Summit Heights Congregation Has Vision Clarity

Located in a mountain lake resort area, Summit Heights was an intentional new congregational expression more than

30 years ago. A sister congregation about 20 minutes away in the county seat town sponsored and launched it. The organizing families included members from this congregation. Some had recently moved to this area, and others wanted something new in their church experience.

The first pastor—Justin Stewart—was an associate pastor from the launching congregation. He led the launch of another new congregational expression earlier in his ministry. Empty nester lay leaders between their late 40s and early-60s composed the core group for the new congregation.

The pastor and core group launched the new congregation with great insight about how to form the congregation and make it one that would last for many decades. Not just one to appeal primarily to the church cultural desires they held as empty nesters, early retirees, or people with a second home in the mountain.

Many early members were in business management or in organizations where planning was an ongoing exercise. Spiritual insight and a desire to continue growing as Christians characterized these founding leaders. Having a low expectation chapel in the mountains did not appeal to the founding leaders. They were a high expectations core group.

Clarity of vision plus spiritual and strategic understandings also characterized the core group. They wished to nurture a model congregation for missional engagement in this exurban location.

They wanted to be the presence of Christ in their context to infuse it with the love of God through Christ Jesus. Their hope was that the rest of the congregation would be captivated by the same motivation.

They understood their community context. The resort community was in an area of great socio-economic diversity which included declining businesses and congregations. As part of their missional engagement, they wished to contribute to their context economically and spiritually. Not just be an island of affluence unconnected with the people who had been there multiple decades.

Connecting with men who sat around the fire at the general store down the mountain from the resort telling stories—while mixing fact and fiction—fascinated them. Addressing the health care desert in the community—particularly for the health needs of women and children—appealed to them.

With this depth and breadth of Christian character, Summit Heights began with an enthusiastic desire to be the presence of Christ in and around the mountain lake resort. Many founding leaders were in the empty nest stage of life and would soon be senior adults. Initially they offered programs, ministries, and services to these two age stages.

They understood the challenges of the *club sandwich generation* composed of empty nest households with one or more older parents who needed their regular attention. Additionally, they had adult children—some of whom had not turned out exactly like these parents intended. Plus, their grandchildren were a focus of their love.

They were the healthiest generation in their multi-generational family in terms of their overall stage of life, spirituality, and emotional maturity. Addressing the needs of the other three generations stretched their time, energy, money, and even their physical stamina. This came at a time they thought they could enjoy a wonderful stage of life. What they discovered were greater family responsibilities that might derail their new congregation if they required too much of their time.

Leaders also understood the necessity to develop early in the congregation's life a focus on three phases of senior adult life—active, inactive, and dependent. As they launched, they started approaches for one of these phases. By their fifth year they had solid programs, ministries, and activities for all three phases.

Summit Heights from the beginning was a high-capacity congregation due to their caliber of leaders. Obviously, they were atypical of new or well-established congregations. From their formation they displayed traits of not only a thriving congregation, but one soaring with faith. They continually looked for the next thing God would lead them to do. They always innovated. They never felt they had arrived and did not need to continue innovating.

Numerically they grew to over 200 in average weekly attendance during their first seven years. The fast development of this mountain lake resort boosted their attendance. This gave them an ability—because of the affluence and generosity of the congregation—to hire staff, develop excellent programs, and construct the essential facilities needed. They had clarity around their mission, purpose, core values, and vision from the beginning of their congregation.

They expressed *Our One Priority* as, *To empower people in the Summit Heights community to experience and share with others the amazing joy of God's Good News.* This priority was the theme of their *Future Story of Missional Ministry* which was a narrative of what the congregation would be like seven years into the future if they with faithfulness, effectiveness, and innovation lived into the call of God for their congregation. They updated this story every year to keep it congruent with their current understanding of God's leadership.

These congregational-wide updating sessions could be tough. Churched culture ideas arose from the broader congregation. Some members were not as deeply committed to soaring with faith as were the core leaders.

The passion and strength of the core leadership would usually prevail. Summit Heights was well on its way to soar with faith as they allowed God to pull them forward into a future known only to Him.

Their Adolescent Years as a Congregation: After a dozen or so years of existence, Summit Heights began to wane in vitality and vibrancy even though they annually updated their *Future Story of Missional Ministry*. During their 14th year—as they had during their seventh year—they engaged in a significant period of re-envisioning God's sense of spiritual and strategic direction. They took a sabbatical in the spirit of Leviticus 25.

They engaged in this process after Justin Stewart, their founding pastor, moved on to another place of ministry. They saw the interim period between pastors as a time to refocus their soaring with faith. They also used the services of an intentional interim pastor to give them time to discern where God might lead them next.

Both congregational and community factors affected Summit Heights re-envisioning in the 14th year. First, many of the empty nesters present since the beginning were now senior adults. Some were no longer as active in the life of the congregation. Second, the community context around their mountain lake resort experienced much growth and significant transition and change.

Third, the homes in the mountain lake resort were beginning to turnover from the first owner to the second owner. They were not only younger than the average congregation member but approached congregational life from a different perspective. Fourth, the founding leaders were aware of too much talk within the congregation of the Summit Heights way of doing things. They knew they needed to change that trend or face a future not nearly as exciting and missionally fulfilling as in previous years.

They took the initiative to call for a major rethinking of the life and ministry of the congregation. They worked hard to get many newer members involved in the rethinking and elected or appointed to key leadership roles in the congregation.

Their efforts worked. The congregation increased its vitality and vibrancy and were once again characterized as soaring with faith. They engaged in specific actions that enhanced the ability to connect with the newer residents. They changed their worship style to include elements more appealing to newer residents. Later they started a second worship service with a fresh style and gave that worship service the prime time to meet on Sunday mornings.

Because of a greater diversity of Christian denominations represented by newer residents, they took the denominational label out of their name and called the congregation Summit Heights Community Church. Further they also affiliated with a second and third national denomination who were compatible with their doctrine and practice.

They found ways to extend their ministry with empty nest and senior adult households into the larger community context to households unlikely to ever attend their congregation. These households needed the ministry focus of Summit Heights in their communities. Economic needs had shifted in the community context to create a larger lower income population. Summit Heights worked with other congregations to create a Christian family ministry organization to serve community needs.

The Years as Twenty-Something: Around their 20th anniversary, Summit Heights committed themselves to rethink the focus, direction, substance, and style of their ministry in a major way. Doing so allowed them to continue soaring with faith year after year.

They developed a multiple month learning process for emerging leaders connected with their congregation. This passed along the heritage and hope of their congregation to this next set of leaders. Among the congregation at-large what they best understood was *Our One Priority* that delineated the ever-evolving focus of the congregation around which people rallied and about which the community knew them.

Clarity Plus Alignment continued to characterize Summit

Heights as a truly exceptional congregation soaring with faith. Summit Height committed themselves to taking a spiritual and strategic sabbatical every seven years to discern once more God's leading and empowering vision.

Soaring with Faith Vision Clarity

"How do you know your congregation has clarity around its vision for soaring with faith?" I asked the group gathering in my home.

No one knew. So, I suggested I could illustrate with the following story.

One day Abby was shopping in her favorite big box store. As she walked down an aisle, she noticed a woman pushing a cart toward her who looked familiar. Then she realized it was a woman who was a guest at her congregation the previous Sunday. Abby met her while serving as a guest services volunteer but struggled in this moment to recall her name.

It appeared the woman also recognized Abby. As they got close and began talking, they laughed about the fact that neither could remember the other's name. They did recall the enjoyable conversation they had the previous Sunday. Abby learned her name was Madison and met 18-month-old Emma, who smiled at Abby from the cart. Madison spoke in glowing terms about the hospitality and worship she and her family experienced.

Just then Elijah, Madison's six-year-old, caught up with his mother. A display of toys had attracted him. Madison said Elijah enjoyed the congregation also and saw a couple of kids he knows from school. Her husband, Jason, was the new family practice physician at the regional hospital's community-based urgent and emergency care center.

The conversation then moved deeper about the congregation. Madison said to Abby, "I am so glad I ran into you. My husband and I were saying last night that it is time to get serious about picking a congregation. We have visited a lot of congregations since moving here. We decided last night that your congregation draws us in. It would really help me if you would tell me what is so special about Summit Heights."

Abby smiled and there was an obvious excitement in her eyes. This was the question she wanted to answer. "Well, at Summit Heights we ..." Then she shared in her own words—not a canned speech—God's empowering vision for her congregation, and ways it is lived out in the congregation, community context, and globally.

The story of Summit Heights impressed Madison. They continued talking a few minutes and then both children were restless so they moved on with the promise they would see one another again soon. They exchanged cell phone numbers so they could connect later.

Walking away, Abby felt great warmth about her conversation with Madison. It was not just that she was able to articulate the church's vision with clarity, enthusiasm, and even pride. It was that Madison represented a younger demographic and seemed to genuinely be interested in the vision of the congregation.

Several days later Abby's small group from Summit Heights met for a family fellowship, and Abby shared about her visit with Madison. She explained the question that led her to share the congregation's vision and its daily impact on her family, the congregation, and the community context.

"Abby," said Brian, "I am dying to know what you said. You have stirred my curiosity."

She then shared what she had said. Again, using her own words and her deep passion for the journey of Summit Heights.

At one point Brian interrupted. "That's it! You are right on target. That is what I also believe. I love our congregation.

Except when I share the vision, I use a different story to illustrate what is meaningful to me and Meg."

Other people spoke up with affirmation. It was obvious this small group had an uncommon and exceptionally strong clarity around the vision and its fulfillment. They all believed deeply in the mission, purpose, enduring values, and vision of their congregation.

Deeply enough they no longer had to repeat a memorized statement or motto to express vision. They had moved beyond this and deeper in their ownership of God's empowering vision for their congregation. They shared with great passion their experience of vision. It was memorable to them and not just a memorized statement.

There is more to understand than just a statement when vision captivates a congregation. It has true clarity and demonstrates great passion. It also focuses its actions on making disciples who make disciples, and those disciples yearn for a world transformed by the unconditional love of God.

Here is a clarity ownership perspective that empowers vision fulfillment:

- When a minimum of 21 percent of the average number of actively engaged adults in the life and ministry of a congregation get the vision, own the vision, seek to live into the vision personally, and engage in disciplemaking actions to fulfill God's empowering vision for their congregation ...

- Whenever the congregation is making a crucial decision, they always—not periodically or often but always—ask the question, "How will this help us fulfill our vision?" Then the congregation is captured by God's empowering vision, and ...

- When living out their clarity of vision, it is not just one of the things these congregations do. It is the one priority around which everything else revolves.

Selected Reflections from the Mentoring Dialogue

"Let me see if I get this right," asserted Roger. "Instead of a short, memorable three- to seven-word mission or motto statement to recite, there is a visionary story that may be recounted in different ways by various people?"

"Yes!" I answered with a huge smile on my face.

Appearing to grind his teeth, Roger replied, "I am going to need more on that. That's going to require some high-powered fertilizer and watering to grow on me. None of my pastor peers do it that way!"

"Let me put it this way," I said as I began a response to Roger.

Regurgitating a memorized mission or motto still requires an understanding of what it means and what actions they are called to take. It primarily remains a left-brained statement with questionable meaning, which is shallow at best.

Instead, your goal should be for people to understand the essence and meaning of your clarity and alignment in the congregation deep enough that they can describe it in their own words and apply it to their personal calling in ministry. The best words they can use are those which form a story of personal ministry.

This means it is not only in their head but also in their heart. When that happens, they are committed to meaningful Kingdom ministry without you having to push them regularly. They are now being pulled forward by the God movement in your congregation.

"George," interrupted Stewart, "What about the phrase you gave me of *Real Denominations Serve Congregations?*"

"Stewart, I have stood by you at one of your national meetings when as pastors walked by you said to them, 'Real Denominations ...,' and they finished the statement '... Serve Congregations.' That means you have sold the sizzle to them, but not yet the meaning and motivation to drive prophetic action."

"Wow! I get it," answered Stewart.

Roger whispered, "Me too! What a great learning."

"You taught that to our pastors of *Soaring* congregations in one of our gatherings with you. That has made a great difference in our movement," added Thomas.

Serving Soaring with Faith Congregations

Convene: *Soaring* congregations are best served by convening with other *Soaring* congregations where they can learn from one another about innovative ministry that takes them further toward their full Kingdom potential. This can be with lead pastors alone, with lead pastors and staff, and with lead pastors, staff, and key leaders. Peer learning is their sweet spot for learning.

Collaborate: Emphasize *Soaring* congregations collaborating in key areas of faithful, effective, and innovative ministry. One specific example I nudged among a group of *Soaring* congregations in Canada was the issue of trading congregational staff between them. At least two principles are at play here. First, where do *Soaring* congregations find staff who already understand soaring with faith? The answer is in other *Soaring* congregations.

Second, where do staff in *Soaring* congregations go to when they are ready to step up to the next level of congregational leadership, but no vacancies exist in their current congregations. Plus, where do you send staff ready to step up so that they can learn new things in a different environment so they can contribute better to helping your congregation soar with faith throughout their ministry. The answer is in other *Soaring* congregations.

Champion Continual Innovation: Periodically invite into *Soaring* congregations individually or at convenings experts who can help congregations think and act on innovations they have not yet thought about or learned how to do. I found even among *Soaring* congregations lead pastors and staff that they had already functioned to a dimension beyond what they knew and had been clueless as to what to do next. Someone outside their system who is knowledgeable can break through the fog for them.

Coaching: *Soaring* congregational lead pastors and key staff can coach other congregations based on what they have learned that works to achieve and sustain soaring with faith. In doing so they gain insight and surprises that help them take their own congregation to a deeper dimension of ministry. In Chapter Eight we will also mention *Soaring* congregations conducting teaching events where they invite people to come learn on-site in their congregation.

Further, lead pastors and key staff of *Soaring* congregations can also benefit from being coached as can all of us. However, it is not as critical for them because of a tendency to be more open to learning how to improve their leadership than pastors and staff in other collectives.

– 4 –

Strong Congregations Focus on Church Growth

*A **Strong** congregation has good clarity about its mission, purpose, core values, and vision. It has excellent programs, ministries, and activities intensely focused on discipleship development and active church membership. It pursues increased church growth through strategic plans it continually updates. Its missional engagement and creative ministry innovations are significant in their impact.*

"I consider my congregation to be very strong. Before hearing your definition and case studies about **Soaring** congregations, I would have said our congregation is one of the best around. I would have put us in the **Soaring** collective. I am still not convinced we aren't. I look forward to hearing what you have to say about **Strong** congregations. If it turns out it is like my congregation, I might want to change your order and say **Strong** congregations are the leading edge congregations."

This was Roger's response to the presentation on **Soaring** congregations as we were gathering for the session on **Strong** congregations. I spoke to his perspective as follows:

"Roger, both **Strong** congregations and **Soaring** congregations are the leaders among all congregations. Between them they account for at least 80 percent of the Kingdom progress made by Protestant Christian congregations. If we were ranking congregations by the strength of their organization and its progress, **Strong** congregations would be the first collective."

"Since we are focusing on empowering Christ-like ministry in communities and among people groups, **Soaring** congregations have greater potential in these areas because of what happens as Christians scatter rather than as Christians gather. Even new congregations can exhibit characteristics of a **Strong** congregation. As you will see later in this session **Strong** congregations can also **Stumble** yet may develop the capacity to be **Strong** again."

Downtown Congregation Launches with Exceptional Worship

This case study addresses the issue of what organizational values are instilled in each new congregation launched. This is a very positive and creative new congregation. What values—**Soaring** or **Strong**—are they most likely to be characterized by new congregations within six months to two years of their life?

Are these values great, good, or questionable?

The Vision: Launching a new congregation two hours away from a parent congregation can be a great challenge, especially if the goal is to have high quality worship from the very beginning. Plus, it may be difficult to connect with a young adult target group who may respond best to high quality sensory worship.

That is exactly what Fellowship Church did with great vision and faith in God's leadership. It sent out a team of young adult ministers and leaders to launch Downtown Congregation. The target city was a fast-growing population area of college, university, and other young adult households. The vision was to launch a congregation which would authentically connect young adults with a Christ-centered spiritual and congregational journey.

The on-ramp could be long, and the outcome uncertain. It was a risk from the beginning. Exceptional worship could not be tightly scripted. Nor would it happen automatically. Could careful design empower participants to sense the presence of God and experience exceptional worship?

Fellowship sought and commissioned four families from their congregation to move to the target city to launch Downtown Congregation. From these four households, Ed, who was on the ministry team at Fellowship, would serve as lead pastor. A professional musician, Andre, would produce the music. Sarah would serve as the small groups coordinator as she did at Fellowship.

Dance and drama were Elizabeth's specialties, and she had a vision for how they would fit into an inspiring worship service. Technology geek and graphic designer Alfredo was excited to contribute his skills. LaDonna's experience was as an event planner and caterer. A weekday preschool teacher, Rebecca, was looking forward to expanding her experience to lead childcare and kid's church.

It was a well-choreographed vision with clarity to launch a new congregation characterized by exceptional worship for young adults.

The On-Ramp: Launching Downtown Congregation was not just about sending four families to a new city with substantial backing from Fellowship. It was about a multifaceted intentional strategy to design exceptional worship for the target audience. Here were the parts. **First**, the families would intentionally live in places where they could connect with young adults. Especially ones who were new residents in the area.

Two families became activities coordinators in apartment complexes as part of the support system for the residents. This strategy at once placed these leaders in contact with people with spiritual needs. The other two families bought homes and moved into new communities where first-time buyers typically lived.

Second, where the launch team worked was intentional. Several launch team members were entrepreneurial and worked virtually. Each connected with a different co-working location near downtown. There they networked with young adult free-lancers. These co-working locations had gathering spaces where the team could huddle on a regular basis.

Third, the team used their vocational experience to network with various businesses, community-based groups, and individuals. Andre sought out other musicians and formed a band that might eventually serve as the praise team. They performed at community events and restaurants. They passed out promo pieces with QR codes about meetups or hangouts.

Elizabeth marketed her services as a drama and dance coach. She coached university students for a ridiculously small fee, and community people at reasonable prices. She sponsored drama and dance groups that had a spiritual focus. Additionally, she got involved in a local theater group.

Alfredo had no problem marketing his website design services and social media skills with young entrepreneurs. He also booked enough gigs with established companies to pay his bills. He offered free introductory classes in computer technology and graphic design in co-working sites.

Referrals and great references from earlier work got LaDonna in the door of organizations to offer her event planning and catering services. She recruited a group of university students to staff events and catering jobs she booked. Her network grew steadily.

All these actions fit well into the small groups Sarah had coached the launch team to start. Once the small groups began growing, LaDonna stepped in and led the team to pull together larger connecting events for small group members and their friends. At first these were medium-size events with 50 to 100 people.

Eventually, and once they found a larger venue, several hundred people would gather for periodic events where Andre's band would play. Elizabeth's groups would perform drama and dance with clear life applications that often stimulated dialogue. Ed would wrap up with a concise takeaway message to get people thinking about Christ-centered life values without an overt churchy pitch.

The Prelaunch: After more than a year of these cultivation activities, Downtown Congregation felt ready to launch. Prelaunch issues abounded. Could they find a place large enough? What day and time would be best to gather? Did they have enough trained and committed volunteers to handle the coordination of large group worship? How would they handle support services such as childcare and kid's church.

A big issue was to be sure the quality of the worship experience met their expectations and those of the young adults attending. Also, worship should clearly point people to God and not just to Downtown Congregation. Would it inspire and represent exceptional worship?

Andre had already put together a music group of first quality instrumentalists and vocalists. The time they spent together gave opportunities for spiritual conversations. Several were not followers of Jesus when he recruited them. A couple did embrace Jesus during the more than a year of lead up to public worship.

Drama and dance teams were ready to go with the tutelage of LaDonna. They, like the music leaders, just needed to know from Ed what the worship themes and key messages would be a couple of months ahead. With this notice they were ready for impactful drama and dance that would cause people to say, "*Wow!*"

Sarah had led the small groups to develop specialties in

various areas such as hospitality and follow-up. With the help of Rebecca, they conducted background checks on the small groups who felt called to handle childcare and kid's church.

Not to be outdone—and it was really a struggle for a nerd like Alfredo—a team focused on technology, light, and sound was ready to go. The monthly worship gatherings had allowed them to work out the kinks. The only issues were whether it would now work in the large retail space they had leased for the public launch. Gremlins are always present in technology.

As lead pastor, Ed suggested the message themes. The whole team worked with him up to a couple of months ahead to decide how they would support that message and even debated with him whether it was on target or not. That led not only to dialogue, but also to intense seasons of prayer to be sure they were God-honoring and not Downtown Congregation promoting. They were not growing a congregation, but the Kingdom. Growing the membership of a congregation would be lagniappe.

The monthly worship gatherings allowed for testing all aspects of the experience. Confident and anxious, they wondered if they could do it every week. They picked up their families and moved to another city to try to do something to impact young adults. Was it going to work?

The Launch: The first Sunday at 5:00 p.m. drew near. Palms were sweaty. Did they have too many chairs set up? Too few? Who knew? Should they have asked people to register for a giveaway to say they were coming? Were they too optimistic or too pessimistic? Anxiety abounded even as they formed a circle, held hands, and prayed just minutes before they opened the doors for the attendees to enter.

The reality is they had done it right. They had not been in a hurry. They had taken more than a year. They had a couple of thousand people in their database with whom they communicated regularly. They had more than 180 people in small groups.

They averaged over 135 in monthly worship experiences for six months. How many would show up?

The answer blew them away—318 people attended their first public worship service. With only minor glitches, all the technology, lights, sound, music, drama, dance, hospitality, childcare and kid's church worked well. Yes, they had been a little pessimistic about numbers. Others would call it realistic. They had only set up 200 chairs. They had lots of chairs, so they were able to adjust.

What people experienced that day was not a worship program or worship service, but a worship experience that left them saying—wait for it—*"Wow!"* Inspirational worship did point people to God. Face-to-face conversations plus social media and online responses revealed people really connected and wanted more.

It was exceptional according to the responses received. People connected with small groups, signed up to volunteer, said they wanted to be involved in community-based ministries Downtown started.

The Test: The launch was on the Sunday following Valentine's Day in 2020 with the theme of God's unconditional love. Four Sundays later the COVID-19 pandemic hit, and live on-site worship stopped.

Three years. It began with praying, dreaming, and planning in Fellowship Church, and the cultivation and readiness of the leadership team for Downtown Congregation. It added up to just over 36 months.

A pandemic was nowhere in their preparation, written plans or recruitment of missionaries to leave their homes and go to the target city.

Inspiring, exceptional worship of our Triune God. Hospitality that instantly connected people to this just now forming community of faith. Excellence unseen by more than 90 percent of all new congregational expressions. Gone? Wasted?

No! They remembered it is about God and not about them. With their calling, passion, talents, and commitment they figured out how to be an inviting and connecting congregation during a pandemic.

It was, indeed, about the worship of God and connecting people to a Christ-centered, faith-based experience. A pandemic called for innovation, not powerlessness. The power emergent out of the exceptional worship of God was greater than the pandemic.

A Break

I called for a break at this point and gave directions about what would be next. "I want to lay out the case study of a long-established **Strong** congregation before we dialogue on this category and talk about how the ten characteristics apply to **Strong** congregations."

Dancing Between Strong and Stumbling

North Main is more than one hundred years old. It is one of the congregations in its southwest U.S. city considered the second most significant congregation of its denomination in the area. It serves with contagious vitality and vibrancy—even soaring with faith during various eras of its ministry.

Several factors contributed to its longevity and soaring nature. One was the generosity of its membership which was able to support the congregation through a Depression, two world wars, and major transitions and changes in its community context.

Second was a series of pastors with capable leadership skills. Strong lay leaders were captured by God's vision for their congregation. An openness to the necessary changes also energized the renewal of their journey.

Third was their willingness to regularly—every seven years—re-envision God's spiritual and strategic direction for them. Plus, they engaged in continual innovation. They never felt like they had arrived. They always knew God had something else for them to do.

Growth Years: Noteworthy during several recent decades was their willingness to allow their lead pastor to have significant authority to make necessary changes in the congregation to empower them to soar once more. He came during a time of lower attendance and diminishing thriving in the life of the congregation. A church growth consultant helped by coaching the pastor and leadership for almost eight years on the steps necessary to thrive.

During this era, the numerical growth of the congregation was steady for two decades until they reached a saturation point in their facilities and parking.

Their facilities did not address the accessibility issues of an aging and mobility challenged congregation. The classroom designs were for a philosophy of Christian education now out of favor. Preschool rooms lacked the space, accessibility, and quality standards parents expected. The sanctuary was not easily adaptable to the use of media, and the special music and drama experiences the congregation wanted to offer.

Parking worked better in a time when many people walked to church. Or if families drove to church everyone was in one car. In recent years, multiple worship services and various volunteer responsibilities meant many households came to this congregation in two or three cars depending on the Sunday schedule and what they attended or volunteered to do.

The neighborhood association tried to restrict on-the-street parking. They filed complaints about the traffic movement on Sundays. These parking factors alone caused a cap in attendance and stalled the numerical progress of the congregation.

It was not that the congregation felt bigger was better. The growth was not as intentional as people thought. It was that they became the congregation of choice for an increasing number of households in their metropolitan area. It was the lack of space, parking, and user-friendly access that turned people away who would otherwise connect with the congregation.

Relocation: These factors led North Main to spend six years moving to a new much more expansive campus on North Main Street seven miles from their original location but in the direction where the majority of their members lived. They also did a total rebranding as their earlier name was Greenwood which described their now former neighborhood location.

That was more than two decades ago.

Not all things were new following their relocation. Programs, ministries, and activities were similar to what they had been in the earlier location. Now there was the ability to handle these efforts. A highly visible location with room for more people and excellent programming drew people in.

Even more so than in their former location, they practiced a church growth model of assimilation of families and households into the culture of the congregation. Parents sought a congregation with programs that would persuade their children to go to church. They sought meaningful spiritual relationships that would help them discover greater meaning in their Christian lives.

It was more of a gathered congregation more than a scattered congregation. Yes, there were ongoing missional projects focused on their context. Yes, there were missions trips to other locations in North American and around the world. But these were more a programmatic offering to members rather than a missional focus of the congregation.

Financially it was a very generous congregation. It put

significant resources into programs, ministries, and activities to attract new people and to deepen people in their relationship with God and North Main. Their priority was clear. It was God first. North Main was, however, a close second. Missional engagement was a lagging third priority.

Transition: The real transition began with the retirement of the long-term pastor. He had led this significant journey for more than three decades. Discovering the next dimension of pastoral leadership took a while.

Many felt the new pastor could not lead them forward. It was unclear if that came out of a lack of vision clarity for continuing to move forward, or from people weary of change who hoped tomorrow would bring a return of yesterday. It may have just been that the next pastor following a long-term, powerful pastor often faces such challenges.

The new pastor led the congregation to embark on a process to move to the next era of church growth. This era was popular during the most recent two decades in congregations throughout North America.

A strong commitment to missional engagement characterized this era. That was clear at North Main. The pastor challenged the congregation to *Live Sent!* Inspired, motivated, and deployed laypersons served with missionary zeal through their discipleship journey. The approach to discipleship that focused on an action then reflection approach was in vogue at North Main.

Generosity Pathways: More than just providing finances to a budget with a heavy emphasis on evangelism, outreach, discipleship, and contributing to missions causes, generosity became a lifestyle. People also gave the gift of time—even making missional engagement their life's focus. Generosity became a lifestyle and not just one element of life in Christ.

To position the congregation for greater generosity, two shifts took place. **First,** the congregation voted to pay off the debt from the relocation with a new capital campaign. This allowed the congregation to rebalance a sizable part of their budget by ending the debt payments. A challenge issued to members called for them to give over three years an amount equal to the tithes and offerings they gave annually. Thus, increasing their contribution by a third during those three years.

North Main also set up a charitable foundation during this campaign and encouraged people to give assets for both short-term and long-term efforts of the congregation. People gave their cars rather than trading them in at a time when used car prices were increasing rather than decreasing.

Financial gifts came from donor advised funds held by families. People of a certain age or greater contributed IRA funds directly to the campaign. A professional financial consultant helped people understand the tax advantages of these non-traditional ways to contribute.

Staff Right-Sizing: Second, the congregation was staff heavy. Over the years they kept employing additional staff to do ministry. Now that the congregation realized the generosity pathway of contributing time, they needed less staff. The congregation shifted to fewer full-time staff and more part-time staff. Teams formed around a full-time staff person with three to four part-time people. The part-time people had a one- to three-year covenant for the role they accepted. Each team had a clear focus. This strategy lowered the overall staff costs.

One of the goals for each staff team was to discover, recruit, train, and deploy volunteer leaders who could assume staff responsibilities. Therefore, staff became coaches of volunteers. Rather than doing things for the congregation, they did things with the congregation.

Within a few years the congregational budget which committed more than three-fourths of its expenditures to staff and facilities—especially with the building debt—was now committing only two-thirds of its income to these areas. Personnel costs were now less than 55 percent of the budget while in earlier years were more than 60 percent.

Not everyone was happy about this shift from the gathered congregation to the scattered congregation. Some also disapproved of de-emphasizing professional ministerial staff with the move to part-time non-ordained people and volunteers.

As of this writing, it is still uncertain whether the transition forward will sustain, or if older, long-term, heavy financial contributors, and powerful leaders will demand the return to the former era. This is a transformation dilemma faced by many congregations.

Soaring with faith may soon be a greater challenge as they deal with organizational issues. In any case, North Main's external image to outsiders was, is, and will be that it is a very strong congregation.

Selected Reflections from the Mentoring Group

I called on Roger and Thomas to weigh in first since they are pastors of what they believe are **Strong** congregations.

Roger began, "When I signed up for this dialogue session, I did so knowing my congregation is a leading-edge congregation. Very strong. Growing—even multiplying. I wanted to learn how we could keep growing. However, already I realize these sessions present a different perspective on how we see congregations. I need time to think this through. I see a lot in this last case study that resonates with the long-term pattern of my congregation. But right now, I still think **Strong** congregations are the best congregations. God is blessing us so much, I do not see how we could in any way be wrong."

"As the pastor of a multisite congregation and mentor to more than a dozen other pastors of similar congregations in our small denomination, I am struggling with this collective," said Thomas. "My struggle is not one of disagreement, but one of how I could have been so wrong for so many years. What you have presented opens up a very different emotional and spiritual understanding of congregational success. Right now, I want to keep learning."

"Now I am really confused," said Chad with a sense of exasperation.

"Before anyone draws any firm conclusions, take a look at how *Strong* congregations come across in the ten characteristics," I said as I passed around the next handout.

"Pay close attention to the characteristics of Expectations. This is a positive factor for both *Soaring* and *Strong* congregations. High expectations are characteristic of congregations where qualitative and quantitative growth happens. The other three collectives have challenges with quantitative growth although selective qualitative growth can still be a positive factor for them."

How are Strong Congregations Addressing The Ten Characteristics?

Clarity: *Strong* congregations have reasonable clarity around their mission, purpose, core values, and vision. They focus more on a motto that pushes their congregation forward than the experience of vision that intuitively guides their journey. Freshening their motto and vision often takes place when it is no longer working for them, or when a new pastor comes. Often their mission, purpose, values, and vision drive their programmatic focus.

Alignment: *Strong* congregations intentionally align their programs, ministries, and activities around the promotional motto that rallies their congregation. They also seek to align their membership for the success and significance of the goal stated or implied in their motto.

People: *Strong* congregations know who they are successful in reaching for active membership and seek to attract more of these same people but may be slow to reach different types of people even as their context diversifies. They may also specifically target geographic communities, or an entire city, metropolitan area, or region in which their people groups are located. Their focus is on what they can plan and do to serve identified demographic groups, and not as much on the communities to whom God is calling them.

Faith: *Strong* congregations involve people in faith formation through a variety of engaging discipleship offerings. In these congregations discipleship is more of a program or curriculum than a process. The difference between discipleship and disciplemaking is that disciplemaking is a process that helps each willing person engage in living into God's calling on their lives rather than simply engaging in missions projects.

Worship: *Strong* congregations focus on worship that is inspiring and a spiritual life celebration for those in attendance. The quality of the music and the proclaimed Word is highly important. A subtle distinction in emphasis between *Strong* congregation worship and *Soaring* congregation worship is that in *Strong* congregations people experience a great worship service, and in *Soaring* congregations they encounter God.

Expectations: *Strong* congregations have high expectations that many members will sign up, participate, volunteer, and even lead the programs, processes, ministries, and activities of the congregation. Further, they expect faithful financial gifts that are either an obedient ten percent tithe of their income, or a significant expression of generosity for those who reject the classic understanding of tithing.

Connections: *Strong* congregations through their clear image of the people group or groups, and the communities to which God is calling them seek to reach out to preChristians, unchurched, underchurched, and dechurched people to engage them in an eternal spiritual journey. They do this out of an understanding that God is sending them out to minister in His name.

Community: *Strong* congregations often mirror the great, in-depth community experienced in *Soaring* congregations. Yet they may also produce a larger number of congregational refugees because they focus too much on successful, growing community experiences. In doing so, they miss the depth of care needed by some people for spiritual, social, physical, and other life needs to be addressed. Their "back door" may be larger than in *Soaring* congregations.

Wellbeing: *Strong* congregations have a clear leadership system which proactively guides positive decision-making and promotes unity within the congregation. The leadership can tend to move from empowering and permission-giving to management and control if multiple issues that could create conflict arise in a short period of time. Their greatest danger is the denial of potential disruptive conflict for too long.

Generosity: *Strong* congregations inspire their members to give sacrificially through the congregation to fulfill the mandate God has given to the congregation. Special promotions are added to an ongoing emphasis on generosity. People are urged to make financial sacrifices, and to invest themselves in the overall mission of God through their congregation.

Selected Reflections from the Mentoring Group

The dialogue following the two case studies and the ten characteristics created the liveliest debate—rather than dialogue—of the whole time this mentoring group was together.

It was good this was the end of the day. I suggested we break for the day and come back tomorrow to talk about *Soaring* and *Strong* congregations.

I had expected this debate. I valued having it. It was a learning experience for me.

Serving Strong Congregations

Coaching: Lead pastors and their key staff of *Strong* congregations can benefit greatly from being coached. Both individual and group coaching. This should be by trained and certified coaches or can involve lead pastors or staff from *Soaring* congregations trained as coaches.

Strong congregational leaders at times do not know what it is they do not know related to the difference between *Strong* congregations and *Soaring* congregations. Some intensity of hubris may characterize these leaders and prevent their congregations from *Soaring*. They need to be challenged about the greater potential they have to be *Soaring* congregations. Coaching is an approach which can add value to their ministry that also affirms their spiritual personhood.

Convene: *Strong* congregations need to convene their lead pastor, staff, and key lay leaders for ongoing learning with other *Strong* congregations. In this case, it is not only peer learning but should also involve facilitation by an outside third party, and guest presenters who can challenge where *Strong* congregations perceive they are as congregations to focus them more on Kingdom growth.

Champion Breakthrough Innovation: *Strong* congregations may perceive they are doing great, they are highly successful, and they just need to learn new actions and tactics which are working for other congregations. This is not true.

They should be challenged to look for the next breakthrough

innovation that will move them to serve as *Soaring* congregations and take them to places in Kingdom ministry they have not yet realized.

Here is a challenging and motivating question which can be posed to them: "What seems impossible today, that if it could happen, would transform the ability of your congregation to realize God's full Kingdom potential for your congregation?"

Make sure any early answers that focus on becoming more successful are cast aside in favor of answers that focus on full surrender to God's leadership.

A Debate Broke Out Over *Strong* Versus *Soaring* Congregations

Fortunately, with the presentation about **Strong** congregations, a day of dialogue was over. Everyone would have an opportunity to ponder overnight the difference between *Soaring* and *Strong* congregations. I announced we would talk it through the next morning.

The next day, while no one was physically injured, a *no-holds-barred* rhetorical debate broke out in my den among the mentoring group. The issue? Well, it was complicated. Everyone had an opinion.

Becky questioned the distinction by asking, "Are not *Soaring* and *Strong* congregations really the same thing?" Chad wondered. "Theologically is not every **Strong** congregation also a *Soaring* congregation? It is the *Strong* congregations I most count on to help me launch new congregations or campuses."

Roger was skeptical. "Can *Soaring* congregations really last very long? Are not all the soft, relational processes of a *Soaring* congregation too weak to sustain themselves?"

From a journalist perspective, Melissa asked, "Is not serving as a *Soaring* congregation so altruistic as to be a fantasy rather than a reality?"

"I challenge that a *Soaring* congregation is better than a **Strong** congregation. Both are congregations of great value to God," was Stewart's answer. Thomas declared, "I want all congregations to be **Strong**. I am not convinced *Soaring* is a higher value in my denominational family."

Everyone had questions or a distinctive perspective. If at this point you are wondering about the difference, you are among friends in ministry. What they did not realize is that I was ready for them. I expected some doubts and a possible debate.

Strong Congregations versus Soaring Congregations ... Which is Better?

Years ago, I was part of an ongoing multi-racial and multi-ethnic gathering of ministers. In one session, a White minister posed a question to a Black pastor. "Pastor, what do you believe is the key difference between White Baptists and Black Baptists?"

The pastor pondered the question a few moments and then said, "White Baptists emphasize being saved, and Black Baptists focus on walking with Jesus."

Although that exchange was many years ago, it still impacts my thinking. It comes to mind when considering the difference between *Soaring* and *Strong* congregations.

The Differences: I recognize multiple possible differences between *Soaring* and *Strong* congregations. I do not see these differences as absolutes. I see them more on a continuum.

Let's identify a baker's dozen key differences and then place them in a continuum exercise for discernment and dialogue. A continuum view is very important for a richer and deeper understanding of and appreciate for the ministry of congregations.

First, is the difference stated by the pastor above regarding salvation and walking with Jesus. *Soaring* congregations focus more on the lifelong journey of walking with Jesus. *Strong* congregations place more emphasis on the event or process of salvation. Certainly, each is concerned about the full continuum of a person's relationship with our Triune God.

Second, *Soaring* congregations place more emphasis on the growth of God's Kingdom as external to the local congregations. Is the community context and/or people groups on whom the congregation is focused becoming more loving and Christ-like? *Strong* congregations emphasize growth of the local congregation as a sign of success.

Third, the pulling of God as He goes before us as we are embraced by his *Missio Dei* or mission of God is more emphasized in *Soaring* congregations. Striving to push forward to make a greater gospel impact is more likely how *Strong* congregations see this.

Fourth, a right-brained *Future Story of Missional Ministry* which is part of a *Spiritual Strategic Journey* is the way *Soaring* congregations imagine their future as they surrender to God's leadership. *Strong* congregations are more likely to engage in a left-brained strategic planning process by which they measure success.

Fifth, a corollary is that *Soaring* congregations are more likely to use discernment processes as they seek to help the whole congregation stay in touch with God's leading. Leadership giving voice to a clear direction is more the pattern in *Strong* congregations. Thus, ownership of the journey is deeper in *Soaring* congregations. While *Strong* congregations create more of a follow-the-leader directional pattern.

Sixth, I would propose there is even a difference in the approach to the Christology theology between *Soaring* and *Strong* congregations. *Soaring* congregations focus on *Who* Jesus was, is, and will be eternally while *Strong* congregations focus more on *What* Jesus did, does, and will do as part of our Triune God.

Seventh, the process of disciplemaking versus the program of discipleship is a key difference. *Soaring* congregations engage followers of Jesus in a lifelong process of growing in the grace and knowledge of Jesus as they are continually maturing in their faith. Gaining knowledge and skills that may also produce spiritual depth through various programs offered to believers tends to be the approach of *Strong* congregations.

Eighth, a challenging biblical interpretation difference between *Strong* and *Soaring* congregations centers around the words "sent" and "received." Is the key message of the New Testament that we are "sent?" Or is it a deeper concept that we need to go to the world's communities and people groups so that they might "receive" the gospel message? My perspective is that *Strong* congregations focus on the people being sent, and *Soaring* congregations emphasize the people who need to receive Jesus as their Savior and Lord.

Ninth, my ministry colleague and friend Eddie Hammett has for decades been one of many proponents of the scattered congregation as needing much of the emphasis we place on the gathered congregation. Both are essential. (See Edward H. Hammett, *The Gathered and Scattered Church: Equipping Believers for the 21st Century*. Smyth and Helwys Publishing, 2015.)

Soaring congregations place more emphasis on the people of God as increasingly scattered in the world to be transformative salt and light. *Strong* congregation tend to measure their effectiveness more on people gathering and place high expectations on attendance growth.

This is a good place for an illustration of this point. Once I heard a pastor talk about dealing with the Sunday sports issue and the attendance of households dedicated to helping their children pursue youth sports.

A deacon in his congregation came to him apologetic that his son's soccer games for the coming season were scheduled for Sunday mornings. His son was a star player and had been with his team for four years. Colleges were beginning to look at him as a scholarship recipient. He did not agree with the scheduling but wanted to support his son.

The pastor suggested the congregation appoint him as a *Marketplace Missionary to Youth Soccer*. The father loved the idea. He was commissioned by the congregation, and he conducted brief devotional services at the soccer field every Sunday morning. He also became the go-to person at the field for people seeking spiritual and life guidance.

Tenth, congregations at their best are living, breathing, moving, and adapting Christ-centered spiritual organisms and movements, rather than institutionalized organizations.

Soaring congregations are more like organisms, and **Strong** congregations are more like organizations. This is a difference in the way congregations functions that must be experienced and felt.

Eleventh, vision clarity is a crucial issue for all congregations. It is one of the places where *Soaring* and *Strong* congregations can be clearly differentiated. Both must have God's empowering vision for their ministry if it is to be one which is faithful, effective, and innovative. How vision is expressed and by whom is a crucial difference between the two types of congregations.

Strong congregations typically have a statement of vision. Perhaps primarily a three- to seven-word motto memorized and regurgitated on cue in public gatherings. Often this is declared by the lead pastor and key leaders. In fact, the concept may be that God imparts vision through the lead pastor to the congregation.

Soaring congregations have an inspiring story that describes the vision God has for their congregation. They believe God imparts vision to the congregation who then builds a story around that vision which even can have unique expressions of it by various congregational participants, yet everyone recognizes it as the vision God has given them. (See Chapter Three and the experience of Abby in the big box store.)

In *Soaring* congregations, it is the hope that the lead pastor is the first or among the first persons to be captured by God's empowering vision for the congregation. This is important because they are the key voice for casting the vision. God is the source of the vision, and the lead pastor is God's servant for casting vision. (I explain this in detail in my book *Captured by Vision: 101 Insights to Empower Your Congregation* which was published in 2017 by WestBow Press but is now out-of-print at my request as I prepare to update it and republish it.)

Twelfth, the order of focused action is a crucial difference between *Strong* and *Soaring* congregations. *Strong* congregations tend to direct focused action to take place, and *Soaring* congregations tend to act and then reflect and focus.

To explain this calls for another congregational story. This is where I began to deeply understand something about the learning process which I had always believed but found a great example in a real congregation.

First Church is in a metropolitan area of around 300,000 people. A military base is present within their area and drives their economics and steady growth. I was invited to consult with them some years ago. It had been ten years since an outside consultant had assisted them with planning that is strategic in nature.

In my first visit with the pastor, we talked about that previous experience with the consultant who was well known to me and an active colleague. The previous consultation was during the pastor's first year at this congregation. The congregation had just celebrated his tenth anniversary when I began consulting with them.

He indicated the congregation had doubled in active membership and attendance during his tenure. They grew from about 250 in average weekly worship attendance to almost 500 during the past decade.

"How did you do that?" was my question to him. Here is what he told me.

I got every able-bodied adult who would, to go on an international missions trip to another continent. We held several orientation sessions before the trip to prepare them for what they would learn and asked them to prayerfully consider during their trip any implications of what they were learning for their personal ministry when they returned home.

Following their missions trip we held multiple debriefing sessions with them to unpack their experience, what they learned, and what they felt God wanted them to do with what they learned.

Then we just sat back and watched amazing things happen within the congregation. No formal new programs. Just encouragement and permission giving for people to try new things.

That's all it took.

Thirteenth, is a focus on the congregational multiplication approaches of *Soaring* and *Strong* congregations. Because of their Kingdom growth mindset, *Soaring* congregations search for overlooked or underserved communities and people groups in and beyond their context. They multiple the Kingdom by launching new congregations who target these communities and groups.

Soaring congregations feel a deep responsibility for everyone around them. They realize when their congregation may have difficulty reaching other socioeconomic, racial, ethnic, and lifestyle groups. Thus, they launch new autonomous congregations among these target communities or people groups.

Strong congregations have a congregational model which works well among clearly defined, somewhat homogeneous demographic groups. They launch new campuses which replicate their successful model in communities and among people groups within their sphere of influence. These campuses are within the same metropolitan area or county, or even a distance away including in other states or provinces.

Long-term these new campuses either remain part of the core congregation's assertive church growth pattern, or they are spun off to become autonomous congregations.

For Review

A **Strong** congregation has good clarity about its mission, purpose, core values and vision. It has excellent programs, ministries and activities intensely focused on discipleship development and active congregation membership. It is pursuing increased church growth through its empowering vision and strategic plans it continually updates. Its missions engagement and ministry innovation are significant in their impact.

A **Soaring** congregation has exceptional clarity and alignment regarding its mission, purpose, and core values. It is captured by God's empowering vision for its full potential focused on Kingdom growth. Clearly present are extraordinary vitality and vibrancy, leadership competency and trust, an external local and global missional focus, an effective disciplemaking process, and creative ministry innovation.

Which is Better? Is it better for a congregation to be **Strong** or **Soaring**? Both are congregations of great value to God's Kingdom. They approach the fulfillment of their mission and vision in unique ways.

My experience tells me **Strong** and **Soaring** congregations together make up 80 precent of measurable Kingdom progress. The other 20 percent is made collectively by **Stumbling**, **Struggling** and **Spiritless** congregations.

A Continuum Between **Soaring** and **Strong** Congregations

No congregation is completely **Soaring** or completely **Strong**. It is appropriate to engage leaders in both of these collectives in discernment and dialogue about how **Soaring** or how **Strong** they are regarding the dozen key differences. Then to talk about and plan for how they believe God is leading them to sharpen the character and nature of how they serve in the midst of His Kingdom.

To engage in discernment and dialogue in a congregation as to whether it is *Soaring* or *Strong*, use the following exercise with staff, lay leaders, or even in an open gathering of the congregation.

I continue to be a learner in this area myself. I am glad to walk your leaders through this continuum if you contact me at BullardJournal@gmail.com.

Here are suggested steps:

1. Present the 13 differences between *Soaring* and *Strong* congregations.
2. Provide each person a copy of the continuum and ask them to place a mark on where along the continuum they believe your congregation is right now. Fully *Soaring* is a 5 on the left, and fully *Strong* is a 5 on the right. Zero would represent an active balance between the two. It does not mean a person cannot decide. They should be encouraged not to mark zero unless they believe there is a clear balance between the two.
3. Then engage in dialogue in small groups if more than a dozen people are completing the exercise, followed by large group dialogue. Skip to full group dialogue if less than a dozen people are completing the exercise.
4. Following dialogue, give everyone a second copy of the exercise, have them complete it based on where they now believe their congregation ought to be. The first time the continuum was scored was their current reality. The second is their idealized intent with insights gained from the dialogue. Then tally the results to discover the overall perspective of the group.

Soaring and *Strong* Congregations Exercise:

Soaring	5	4	3	2	1	0	1	2	3	4	5	Strong
Walking with Jesus												Conversion
Kingdom Growth												Church Growth
Pull												Push
Spiritual Strategic Journey												Strategic Plan
Discernment												Leader Directed
Who												What
Disciple-making												Discipleship
Received												Sent
Scattered												Gathered
Organism												Organization
Visionary Story												Motto Statement
Action Reflection												Directed Action
Multiply with Congregations												Multiply with Campuses

Selected Reflections from the Mentoring Group:

"This convinces me. I am already thinking how I might help launch new congregations which are *Soaring* from the very beginning," exclaimed Chad. "The case study you shared during the session on *Strong* congregations—I believe it was Downtown Congregation—had me thinking that was a high bar and role model for the ideal new congregation launch. However, now I realize that in spite of their excellence it might not end up being a *Soaring* congregation."

Stewart weighed in and said, "It does make a good case for *Soaring*, but before I say I agree, I want to use the test exercise you have given us and try it out with some of my congregations. I certainly agree Mount Calvary which you talked about yesterday is a *Soaring* congregation, but I need more than one example to affirm a pattern."

"My issue remains how long can a congregation remain *Soaring*. When I get back home, I want to look at the long-term pattern of congregations in my network. I will still need some convincing a congregation can sustain the *Soaring* characteristic for more than two or three years," was the judgment of Roger.

"Roger, my response is five to seven years," I suggested. "I believe in the seven-year sabbatical pattern. If a congregation does not take a deep look at the vitality and vibrancy of his direction every five to seven years, they will digress in effectiveness and excellence."

– 5 –

Stumbling Congregations Lack Vision But Have Potential

*A **Stumbling** congregation needs clarity and alignment about its mission, purpose, core values, and vision. Management of programs, ministries, activities, plus financial and facilities resources are their focus. The leadership wants a short-term fix but may not achieve a long-term solution. They need a spiritual and strategic journey but do not have the necessary readiness for change. They lack the capacity to be **Strong** or **Soaring** yet wish they could achieve it.*

"With this session we will move to talking about the 80 percent or more congregations in North America who are neither *Soaring* nor *Strong*," I said opening this session. "Yet with discontinuous, disruptive, and destructive change efforts could be *Strong* or perhaps one day *Soaring*.

For even the highly motivated *Stumbling* congregations it could take five to seven years not only to fully change their direction, but to solidify that new direction into their permanent culture. Too often we declare a turnaround congregation successful too quickly."

Chad held up his hand and declared, "That is why I like

launching or relaunching congregations! We know in the first two or three years if it is going to be a great congregation."

"Hold on, Chad," interrupted Thomas." The campuses I launch, and new congregations I work with other congregations to launch are not quite a sure thing for the five to seven years George is talking about. It does take longer for them to solidify their own culture and leading-edge focus."

"OK folks, let's move on to talk about *Stumbling* congregations. We can settle that debate in a different gathering," I interjected to move us on and not get mired in a controversial topic.

Out of Focus: Stumbling Congregations Often Lack Vision

Several years ago, I stumbled while walking down the steps from my office on the second floor of my home. I was looking down and reading a paper I was holding. My feet got tangled, and I fell down the last seven steps. I landed on the floor by the front door.

My fall made a loud bang. My wife came running afraid I was terribly hurt. I was not. Nothing was broken. I just had a bruise or two and a stupid look on my face.

I was not paying attention to where I was headed and what I was doing.

Not Paying Attention: *Stumbling* congregations have a similar experience. They stop paying attention to where they are headed and what they are intentionally doing to get there. Then they stumble. God's vision that once empowered their spiritual and strategic journey is no longer impactful. Their actions focus on preservation of what they have done in the past.

Rather than focusing on their future with intentionality and innovation, they keep doing the same things—over and over—and expecting different results. This sounds like insanity to many people looking at them from the outside, but to them it seems natural. It is about the things they love to do and want to keep doing. They believe they must just push harder.

The reasons their programs, ministries, and activities are not working anymore are a mystery to them. Their community context has changed, but they believe the new residents ought to respond to what they are offering.

They cannot understand why young families with children no longer connect with their congregation in large numbers as in past years. Even their own adult children and grandchildren may have moved to different congregations.

Not Captured: A *Stumbling* congregation is not captured by God's empowering vision. Management of programs, ministries, and activities, plus financial and building resources are their focus. Their lay leadership wants a short-term fix, not a long-term solution, and may consider changing pastors. They actually need a new vision for their spiritual and strategic journey but lack the necessary readiness to be captured by God's empowering vision.

Many *Stumbling* congregations were once *Strong* or even *Soaring* congregations with a clear vision supported by programs, ministries, and activities that were well aligned to fulfill their vision. When their context changed, and the average age of their congregation member was older, they did not engage in continuous innovative transition and change. So, they plateaued and then declined.

Their response was to push harder to do the things that once worked rather than asking God to reveal a fresh vision for a new season of ministry. Pushing harder increased their decline and encouraged the growth of spiritual insight cataracts that hindered their ability to see God's future for them.

They often measured success by how well their programs were doing and whether they were reaching their budget. They kept expenditures within their budget and did not use the reserve funds they had saved for the proverbial *rainy day* that seldom happens.

Many **Stumbling** congregations delay routine maintenance and watch their buildings and grounds slowly deteriorate. Empty classrooms become storage rooms. Guest parking becomes senior adult parking.

Or they do the opposite. They continue upgrading their facilities and grounds to make them look more appealing. They call on the financial faithfulness of their members and use the *if we build it, they will come* approach to provide a fellowship or recreation building, preschool and children facility or some other structure they believe will inspire the congregation and attract new people.

Not Ready? **Stumbling** congregations fantasize about once again serving as a **Soaring** or **Strong** congregation, but they are not ready. They have a vision of the past with programs, ministries, and activities positioned to recreate the past.

They are the congregations who would be ready if the 20th century returns tomorrow. Until they are willing to admit this, they cannot move forward. The peer learning communities and coaching processes that help **Soaring** and **Strong** congregations take their next steps in ministry will not work for these congregations.

They need a change of heart and direction. They need answers to questions they do not know to ask. They need outside consulting, coaching, or help with a relearning approach for the next seasons of ministry. They need to visit congregations who were once **Stumbling** but have discovered and sustained a way forward. This requires resource people experienced with working with **Stumbling** congregations who are sponsored by denominations or parachurch ministries.

Here is an example of a **Stumbling** congregation who did recover, has great ministry at this juncture, but still is not what they once were. Past glory has partially but not completely returned as their context is now very different.

Lake Avenue Shifts from Programs to People

An intentional new congregational expression 65 years ago, today Lake Avenue is a congregation wanting to soar with faith. Success and significance escape them. In certain ways it is a high quality congregation with a passionate group of ministers and lay persons. They seek to serve as Great Commandment people who love God, love one another, and love their neighbors.

The vision for launching Lake Avenue focused on the fast-growing outer edge of a larger metropolitan area. Seven decades earlier its county had a population of less than 100,000. In recent years, its county passed the one million population mark.

When Lake Avenue began it was an attempt to capitalize on the fast-growing suburban areas around the central city of their county. It successfully responded to a wave of population growth. During its first generation of life, it grew to a weekly worship attendance of more than 1,200. Religious leaders in the area called them a model of suburban family ministry which others should study and emulate.

Change Happened: Several factors changed them within a short timeframe. An unethical ministry action ensnarled the pastor. Their flagship weekday children's ministry experienced an internal moral failure. These two incidents caused congregational members and community families involved in the ministries of the congregation to withdraw.

Beyond these internal issues, the churching patterns of their area shifted in significant ways. The fast growth of their metropolitan area moved out beyond their location, their denomination started more new congregations to connect with this growth. Fewer households sought out Lake Avenue as their congregation of membership. Further, it was a place of mobility for households. Its location attracted many professional and academic households from throughout the world who often brought with them different approaches to faith and spiritual practice.

A new, rapidly growing contemporary congregation sprung up within two miles of their location and reached an attendance of 2,500 within its first decade. Then a multi-campus mega congregation from an adjourning county started a new campus within a half mile of the Lake Avenue's location.

This collection of events resulted in Lake Avenue declining from an attendance of more than 1,200 to less than 500 within a decade. At this low attendance point, a new pastor came to the congregation who had years before served as an associate pastor before moving on to serve as lead pastor in other congregations.

Right-Sizing: He knew Lake Avenue needed a fresh start. Before that could take place, it would be necessary for the congregation to *right-size*. Even though they were much smaller than their attendance a decade ago, they still wanted to support the programs, ministries, and activities of previous years. They even kept the same size staff as during that former period. To pay this staff they used reserve funds.

It was impossible to sustain the programs, ministries, and activities due to the significant decrease in lay volunteers available to provide leadership and followership. Some programming died, became mediocre, or was kept alive by staff members seeking to justify their jobs. They struggled to keep the programs, ministries, and activities alive.

Several years into a transformation effort, Lake Avenue shifted from thinking about having enough staff for programming, to thinking about what volunteers they must have to lead essential programming. It took multiple steps to transition from a programmatic approach to discipleship led by staff, to the process of disciplemaking led by laypersons.

Their first step reduced staff by 40 percent. It then took more than a year for the congregation to recover from that relational blow to people who were best friends with staff persons affected by the *right-sizing*. This effort did bring staff to a size within annual budget funds, which was an essential move, but it took a while for the congregation to accept this. Some could not. Attendance decreased again.

Spiritual Strategic Journey: Step two engaged the congregation in a year-long process known as Spiritual Strategic Journey. The process empowered the congregation with a *Future Story of Missional Ministry*. This story imagined what the congregation would be like seven years into the future if they with faithfulness, effectiveness, and innovation lived into the call of God on them.

The *Future Story of Missional Ministry* is a narrative that can tell or imply the congregation's discernment of God's empowering vision for them. In the case of Lake Avenue, their vision focused on being a disciplemaking congregation on mission for Christ.

The journey focus launched from their Spiritual Strategic Journey process was on target. Yet, the effort needed to live into their future story was still daunting. Knowing where they felt God was leading them involved even more adjustments than those of a couple of years earlier.

First, they adjusted how they did programs, ministries, and activities based on convening a lay group who would lead them and connecting staff persons who would coach them. Second, re-evaluation of staff roles to connect the best staff role with each lay group called for major adjustments again. Third, some staff did not fit the role of coach, even following training in coaching, and moved on to a different ministry role outside of Lake Avenue.

Five-Year Recap: Five years after the Spiritual Strategic Journey process, significant progress could clearly be measured. The number of programs in the congregation was about the same because several ineffective and overly staff-driven programs no longer existed. Replacing them were lay initiated programs that fit the future story of the congregation.

A symbol of the new day at Lake Avenue revolved around the rewriting of staff position descriptions to transition to be coaches. Staff were obviously faithful and effective in their service. Yet, they were so accustomed to staff leading everything that they struggled with laypersons leading an increasing number of things. Their role was now to coach laypersons rather than leading laypersons.

During a transition period, staff participated in Christian leadership coaching training. This attempted to provide an opportunity for them to reset their personal leadership style. It worked for some staff and not for others.

Ultimately, staff were invited to accept a new position to fulfill specific parts of the *Future Story of Missional Ministry*. Between matching staff calling and skills with the new position descriptions and evaluating their response to using a coach approach to leadership, not every staff person was offered a new position. Those who were not offered a new staff position were helped to transition to their next place of ministry.

They used a leadership community for communication, correlation, and collaboration among the lay leaders with the staff serving as coaches and liaison to the administrative support available to the teams guided by the lay leaders.

Selected Reflections from the Mentoring Group:

"Several congregations near my congregation have been in situations like Lake Avenue. But none of them have been able to make the necessary changes to live a new life of vitality and vibrancy," was Roger's initial response to this case study. "I have watched these congregations, and at times at night I utter that overly used phrase, 'There but for the grace of God ... .' I am encouraged to hear this story, but I wonder how much conflict they went through to engage in right-sizing their staff."

I responded as the consultant who worked with this congregation both in the staff downsizing and the Spiritual Strategic Journey. "It delayed their turnaround more than a year and resulted in losing more than 100 more members. But long-term it worked. The process from beginning the staff right-sizing to getting traction for the turnaround was three years. Delayed gratification is a key part of dealing with *Stumbling*, *Struggling* and *Spiritless* congregations."

"This was my congregation," said Becky quietly and tearfully.

"Oh, I am so sorry, Becky," Chad said as he put his hand on her shoulder. "I'm sorry your congregation has experienced this same thing."

"No, you don't understand. This was my congregation that George worked with. That is why I am here to learn more about *Soaring* and *Strong* congregations so we can continue our journey," Becky said, as tears rolled down her cheek. "I was the chairperson for both processes."

What Are the Characteristics of Stumbling Congregations?

Clarity: *Stumbling* congregations lack clarity around their mission, purpose, core values, and vision. They are uncertain about who they are and where they are headed. They realize this and want to do something about it, but they are not sure what or how to engage a new spiritual and strategic journey. Programs, ministries, and activities may function in a high-quality way.

Their assumption is that the current or new pastor will bring vision to them.

Alignment: *Stumbling* congregations do not have an empowering vision around which to align their programs, processes, ministries, and activities. They align what they do around their cultural understanding of congregations. While they engage in planning, try some new programs, and do some innovation of their tactics as an attempt to strive for the success of their congregation, they still have no vision.

People: *Stumbling* congregations focus on reaching the type of people they have been reaching in previous years. These may either be people nearby or certain demographic target groups. If their community context is changing, they are slow to adjust the focus of their efforts. They realize they may not be reaching the next generation and that the average age of people in their congregation is increasing.

Faith: *Stumbling* congregations offer programs of faith formation in keeping with their denominational or network tradition. Periodically a disciplemaking process is present in *Stumbling* congregations, but that requires effort that is uncommon within their fellowship. The focus of their faith formation efforts is often more about fellowship and support than spiritual progress.

Worship: *Stumbling* congregations have an established pattern of worship which they seek to repeat each Sunday. People expect various elements of worship to take place with a certain style. They expect a certain order of worship and get confused when things do not happen in that order. Worship is not about the new thing God might do in and through them, but the reliable things they can experience in worship each Sunday.

Expectations: *Stumbling* congregations have three clear categories of expectations. These categories are present in *Soaring* and *Strong* congregations, but more clearly reveal themselves in stuck congregations. Pastors and staff are expected to be "all in." Elected and appointed leaders are expected to set the example for the congregation. The rest of the congregation is expected to do the best they can to fulfill the mission while lacking a vision.

Connections: *Stumbling* congregations respond to people who seek to connect with their congregation. Non-members often need to take the first step. The congregation is not proactively reaching out to new people except through events—often at the church facilities—to which they expect non-members to come and express interest in connecting with the congregation.

Community: *Stumbling* congregations, particularly where the average member has been connected for 15 to 20 years or more with the congregation, unintentionally create levels of community. Many of their formal or informal community or small groups feel like they are closed to new people. New, sustainable, caring community must be created with people who connected during the last six months for in-depth community to thrive throughout the congregation.

Wellbeing: *Stumbling* congregations are hampered in developing and maintaining wellbeing systems because they lack clarity around mission, purpose, core values, and vision. Competing visions and conflicting ways to live into these visions can divide the congregation. Not only the denial of conflict for too long, but also the lack of a process for engaging conflict can move them from being *Stumbling* to *Struggling*.

Generosity: *Stumbling* congregations often have a classic commitment to tithes and offerings. They may still use an annual stewardship promotion campaign to raise the budget. They are also experiencing more designations than in years past as people want to support specific efforts. They have difficulty getting younger generations to commit to traditional giving pattern, but they will support special appeals for specific purposes.

Trinity Could Only Reach Their Kind of People

Trinity Congregation was the original congregation of its denomination in what was then a crossroads called Grandview outside a major metropolitan area in the western part of the U.S. For decades it was the only congregation of its denomination within a nine-mile radius. It was also the only congregation of any denomination with more than 100 people in attendance.

Four families, who were descendants of the original European settlers in this part of the country, were the permission-givers for everything happening in the congregation. They all engaged in agricultural endeavors, with each owning hundreds to thousands of acres of land and thus controlling any new development whether residential, commercial, or industrial.

One North-South and one West-East road ran through the area, plus farm to market roads. Trinity was located near the intersection of the two main roads.

For a century, Trinity served as the dominant congregation in the area. Commercial and industrial developments that primarily served the needs of agriculture businesses joined Trinity along the road soon after World War II. Residential development began when farming families sold their land.

Trinity was 13 miles from the center of what became a major metropolitan area in the last half of the 20th century. The central city of that area was the transportation hub for farming products both from the farm to various markets, and from the factories to the farms. Due to the large amount of farming in the region, central city became not only a transportation hub, but a trading marketplace and a financial center. Additionally, a land grant university began to experience tremendous growth which drew other businesses to the area.

The metropolitan area grew to where it had the largest population concentrated in a 150-mile radius. While all of this happened, there sat Trinity. Functioning in the same way it had for a century, it was still the congregation to attend if you had heritage in the area.

Dramatic Change: Then dramatic change happened in their context.

For decades government entities debated the location of a beltway to encircle the metropolitan area. The longer they debated, the further out the location of the beltway became. Eventually it moved so far out that it was past Grandview. When the route of the beltway was announced, this created a boom for Grandview. Residential and commercial development took place for four decades until the area around Grandview was saturated.

Trinity's facility became dwarfed by the development around it. Small neighborhoods that began before this boom became hidden by the new communities dotting the landscape. The demographics of the area changed from small town to major suburbs. From blue collar to white collar. From working class economically to middle to upper middle class, and with some emerging affluence.

The development moved beyond the new beltway with new communities on the other side of what became a barrier to attract new members for congregations like Trinity who were inside the beltway.

A couple of innovative yet traditional congregations inside the beltway relocated to outside the beltway. New congregations, primarily with a contemporary style, launched around the emerging communities outside the beltway.

Population Explosion: Almost 75,000 people over four decades moved to within a five-mile radius of the congregation. The number of cars that passed in front of Trinity's facilities numbered in the tens of thousands. Trinity just sat there.

During the three of the four decades of the development the same pastor led the congregation. He was as committed as were his lay leaders to hoping that tomorrow would bring a return of yesterday. While they did reach a few new families moving into the area, those they reached had a certain set of characteristics.

Their mindset was blue collar. They grew up in the type of congregation represented by Trinity and were churched culture households. They knew how to provide programmatic leadership for a congregation like Trinity. They wanted a congregation like they had back home but had moved to this area for employment. They were two-income households as that is what it took to live in this area.

The new families connecting with Trinity helped keep its identity as a churched culture enclave. They liked the way the facilities of Trinity looked inside and outside as that also matched what they knew from their past. They were fine that the older people controlled the management of the congregation as that meant they had fewer meetings to attend at night when they got home from work.

While they knew everyone ought to be a Christian, they had little or no experience in how to share their faith. Disciplemaking that came from a process of spiritual formation was not part of their heritage. Congregational programs and their success were their heritage.

While they wanted Trinity to grow—especially with younger families—they were not sure where they would sit. The worship center was full. The Christian education rooms were full. The fellowship hall was full. They were landlocked and constructing a new building without tearing down an existing building was not an option. The older generation was not letting go of their money for fear they would need it.

The pastor serving Trinity had his heart in the right place about Christian ministry. He was about the Good News of Jesus. He wanted everyone to know Jesus. But he was unsure of himself and afraid to connect with people not from his cultural background.

He preached an evangelistic message every Sunday. He urged people to come forward at the end of the service to receive Jesus as their Savior. As people looked around, they realized that other than children coming of age that everyone was "saved." Yet they loved the emphasis of their pastor. Again, it reminded them of church as it ought to be.

The question for Trinity was, "How is our congregation connecting with new people?" Not very well was the only truthful answer. Yes, they connected with the families from a similar background, but not much beyond that.

If people sought them out and asked for spiritual guidance or gave testimony of an emerging Christ-centered life they were glad to respond. The congregation provided spiritual mentoring for these people. The key was that these people sought them rather than being sought by Trinity. Serving as the gathered congregation rather than the scattered congregation was Trinity's pattern.

A high priority was the spiritual cultivation of children born into and growing up in the congregation. Parents focused on this. Congregation leaders rejoiced in this. They wanted strict, biblical standards taught to their children. The public schools were "godless" in the eyes of some laypersons. Because of the need for two incomes in the household, few families home schooled, so they want their congregation to deprogram what their children were learning in school.

Great rejoicing took place when an individual or family transferred their membership to Trinity from another congregation. Here were churched culture people who knew how to actively take part in congregation life and supply financial support. In the future—once they had earned the confidence of current leaders—they might serve in a leadership role, but not initially. They had to earn the right to lead.

Leadership Transition: Retirement arrived for the pastor who had served the congregation for 30 years. When he set his retirement date, he also urged the congregation to use denominational resources to plan a new strategy for the future.

He knew during his 30 years the congregation had ignored the dramatic changes and population explosion to hang on culturally to the past rather than to embrace the future.

He knew as he had sufficient self-awareness to realize he had not led the congregation to address the transitions and changes around them. It was not who he was. He could not lead a different kind of congregation.

He understood that while the congregation needed a disruptive innovation pattern, they could now be ready for it. Some opportunities may have passed them by since population growth was now out beyond the bypass.

He knew although the congregation needed a different direction, while he was present, he could not allow the developing strategy to negatively reflect on his decades of leadership. To prevent this, he tried to control the planning process.

The lay leaders knew the children and teenagers needed a vastly different program strategy. They also understood it was not going to happen if the current pastor remained as pastor. They realized their best plan was to stall any new strategy until the pastor retired. They did this. Then they rallied support for a vastly different future for the congregation.

They knew the next pastor must be younger, open to disruptive innovation. At the same time, the next pastor must be able to gain the confidence of the congregational leaders 65 or more years old.

The long-term pastor retired. A new strategy was set. A younger pastor arrived. New, innovative actions began. An initial increase in attendance resulted in 20 percent growth in participation. A new worship service accommodated the increased attendance.

The Explosion: Then it happened. Twelve to 18 months into the tenure of the new pastor. What was it? What is your guess?

The descendants of the four founding families still controlled Trinity. Only their kind of people were welcome.

The congregation experienced a split between people who supported the four founding families and the heritage of the congregation, and the people who felt it was mandatory for them to respond to the new realities of their context. Within a few years Trinity slipped from *Stumbling* to *Struggling*.

In the midst of this story many people thought about but did not speak up about the land the four families owned and how in their selling of it they could have benefited the congregation in multiple ways but did not.

Selected Reflections from the Mentoring Group

"There are certainly more Trinity's than there are Lake Avenues in the stories I write," sighed Melissa as the room went quiet. "In fact, the same thing can be said about denominations. Few are getting a fresh vision and realigning their structures to empower it."

Stewart shook his head and shared, "There are more Trinity's in my denomination than I can count. The average age of the people who attend on Sundays in these congregations is often 60 or more. *Stumbling* congregations moving toward *Struggling* are the fastest growing group of congregations we have. In many of them the pastor does not have enough money in savings or annuity plans to retire. He will have to keep preaching until he cannot go on or joins the host of heavenly witnesses."

"Unfortunately, all Protestant Christian denominations do an inadequate job of helping *Stumbling* congregations address the long-term vitality and vibrancy while they still have resources and opportunities to develop a fresh vision and impactful strategies," I noted for the group.

"Congregations which were once *Soaring* or *Strong* need not only preventative actions, but also proactive actions when they become *Stumbling.* Every denomination I know waits until they are *Struggling* or *Spiritless* to engage in what they call revitalization or replanting. I have two things to say about that.

"Denominations wait until it is too late for many types of responses to work. Second, they need to help congregations during what I call the lost years of congregations which actually begin when they are *Soaring* or **Strong.** Enough evidence is present early on that point to the future *Struggling* of congregations."

Serving Stumbling Congregations

An Overview: The typical *Stumbling* congregation needs new clarity and alignment. They often rely on their previous clarity and alignment long past its effectiveness. It is not working for them. It likely has not been working for them for a number of years already.

However, they are congregations with many good qualities which mask the fact they do not know who they are any more and where they are headed. A smaller percentage of what they do is working effectively for them.

Once congregations are *Stumbling*, they need to once again be captured by a new empowering vision from God. They must be willing to lay their current understanding of where God is leading them on a sacrificial altar and seek a new sense of direction from our Triune God.

The depth of transition and change they must have is discontinuous. They should interrupt their current spiritual and strategic journey and discern a new journey.

Measuring Vitality and Vibrancy: Congregations often fail to measure several statistics that reveal their true status. First, the average age of the average attending adult has been creeping higher for a number of years. In many congregations the average age of attendees goes up annually. They are slowly becoming an aging congregation.

Second, the distance or time people travel to attend worship increases each year with more people living farther away than previously. Once the travel time reaches twenty minutes or more people are less active and may be looking for a closer congregation. One corollary to this is the average travel time people commute to their work or big box store shopping may create a limit of the amount of time they will travel to attend worship.

Third, the length of time people have attended a congregation increases annually. The ideal for long-established congregations is for half the attendees to be engaged with the congregation for ten years or less, and half for ten years or more. When this number exceeds fifteen years it is problematic for congregations.

Fourth, the manner in which people become members of the congregation shifts. Consider three:

(1) Transfer Growth: People move their membership to a congregation from another congregation.

(2) Biological Growth: Children and adults from households where at least one adult is already a Christian, and a member of a congregation, become Christians and join the congregation. Think about this one. Some people want to debate that these are new Christians and should fit the third category below. Yes, they are. However, I stand by this definition as it makes a crucial difference in the long-term growth of congregations when they are reaching totally non-Christian households.

(3) Evangelistic Growth: People from non-Christian households accept Jesus as their Savior and Lord and join the congregation. This is the cutting edge of new growth and long-term vitality and vibrancy.

Here is the key impact of knowing this figure. When less

than ten percent of the new people who connect with a congregation annually are the result of evangelistic growth, the long-term pattern of the congregation may be plateau and decline. It is certainly rapidly headed to become an overly churched culture congregation.

Fifth, is to understand the length of membership of people who hold congregational elected, appointed, and even highly impactful volunteer roles. This is another place where the ten-year figure is important to know. At least half of the people filling these roles need to have been members for less than ten years. Or teenagers who have become adults serving in the congregation within the past ten years.

Certainly, there are other measurements besides these. Other collectives of congregations are also impacted by these. But *Stumbling* congregations are where the impact of these measurements begin to be significantly felt.

With these things in mind, here are three approaches for external helping agents to assist *Stumbling* congregations.

Consult: Unlike in *Soaring* and *Strong* congregations where enough resources and innovative ideas are circulating, new information and insights are needed for *Stumbling* congregations. Therefore, an outside expert approach using a consultant who begins with an assessment and then moves to an intervention is necessary in these situations.

Also, the resistance to transition and change may be sufficiently high in these congregations that the consultant needs to understand the dynamics of conflict and trauma in congregations to help them move in a new direction.

Content: A corollary to the need for an assessment and intervention approach is that the consultant needs to be able to bring to the congregation, or broker for them, new content, methods, programs, ministries, and activities which fit their situation. Ones for which they already have essential leadership, or this leadership can be easily developed.

The new or renewed content, methods, programs, etc., will often need to be implemented in stages over a period of years.

Champion Congregational Case Studies: *Stumbling* congregations often do not know about congregations who were *Stumbling* yet were able to chart a path forward and transform. They need to explore possible case studies and then schedule on-site visits to several of these to talk with the pastor, staff, and lay leaders about their journey.

It is hard for them to imagine what the transitions and changes they need to take would be like. Reading an article or book about these congregations may not suffice, and some on-site case studies could be about something that happened many years ago. This is a place where denominational staff can help them discover captivating case studies.

STRUGGLING

– 6 –

Struggling Congregations
Want a Silver Bullet

*A **Struggling** congregation is smothered by their overly churched culture with an internal focus on making tomorrow a return of yesterday. The direct, dramatic, divine intervention of God is their faithful hope. They struggle to keep their programs, ministries, and activities functioning at a vital and vibrant level. The core of the congregation are often empty nesters and senior adults. They want to know what to do next year rather than taking a long look at their situation.*

"In this session we will move to talking about congregations who not only lack vision, but also no longer have a significant, congregational-wide commitment to making disciples. Their programs are declining and disappearing partially because of a lack of leaders," I said to introduce **Struggling** congregations.

"Also, these congregations—perhaps more than any other collective of congregations—are asking their denomination for help. They are out of answers and want—actually they demand—answers from their denomination."

"Yes, I know these congregations well," said Chad. "We cannot get them to do anything to change their direction, even though we offer them various strategies. What we offer is not the Silver Bullet they want. However, we can get them to nest new congregations of a different racial, ethnicity, or socioeconomic status in their facilities."

"Interesting," said Thomas. "I had not thought much about using the facilities of these congregations for church planting. In our small denomination we let these congregations fade away. We just do not have anything for them. Perhaps we need to rethink this."

Melissa spoke up saying, "A majority of the stories I write are about what is happening to congregations when they have lost their way and are significantly declining."

"One more thing before we dive into a case study," I said. "More than 90 percent of *Struggling* congregations are plateaued or declining, with the largest percent of these congregations declining. Their traditions and managing them are in control. Very little innovation is taking place."

A Congregation on the Edge of Christianity Struggles with Direction

"Daniel, this congregation is yours. They have followed you on your wandering theological journey away from core Christian beliefs. Now what are you going to do with them?"

These were my words to a pastor in a major urban area of North America one Saturday afternoon when he was home for the weekend from his sabbatical study. He was attending a progressive seminary for a semester for time away his congregation granted him during his seventh year of ministry among them.

His study focus was on Buddhism, other Eastern religions, and their positive impact on Christian theology. I have always laughed and told people this was certainly not a core Christian gospel issue, but it was the one he passionately wanted to pursue.

He responded, "I know I am on a very progressive Christian

journey away from the center of faith, but I never intended the congregation would follow me on that journey."

Chuckling I said, "What did you expect them to do? You delivered essays on Sunday mornings for more than six years, then printed and distributed them throughout the congregation. When I used an exercise in focus groups giving people three choices of purpose statements for the congregation, overwhelmingly they chose the one I crafted from reading some of your essays. They now believe what you believe is the purpose and focus of this congregation."

This First Church was around 100 years old. During the third decade of their life, they constructed an 800-seat sanctuary. Their pastor at that time was a nationally known preacher. They filled the sanctuary every Sunday.

A half century later they stopped worshiping in the sanctuary. Their numbers had dwindled to under 100. They moved to a portion of their building known as the Living Room. It had a baby grand piano in it, a large fireplace, was wonderfully decorated, and could seat 60 to 65 people within it.

Next to the Living Room was a room called the Dining Room followed by a Kitchen. It literally felt like a home. Large beautiful wooden pocket doors adorned the opening between the Living Room and the Dining Room.

As long as attendance was less than 65, the pocket doors were kept closed. It provided a warm sense of community closeness during worship. However, three times in the past ten years, attendance had grown beyond 65 and the pocket doors were open for worship, at least for a while.

Longtime core members of the congregation did not like when this happened. From out of nowhere, when weekly attendance grew to 75 to 85, some incident would happen, then up to 30 people would get frustrated and leave the congregation. The pocket doors could once again be closed. This happened three times in the decade before I began consulting with this congregation.

While this congregation was certainly more progressive than almost all congregations I was privileged to serve as a consultant, I like to tell their story. They were also making a very clear and unique contribution to the Christ-centered faith journey of spiritual seekers on the edge of Christianity.

It had to do with several very distinct clusters of people who attended. First, were the *Keep the Pocket Doors Closed* people. There were long-term members who were all senior adults, and a few of their close friends who liked to attend worship with them.

Second, was a cluster of empty nest and early retirement households. They were committed *Christian Church Culture Households*, who held some of the key leadership roles in the congregation.

Third, was a group of people if you asked them if they were Christians, they would say they were *Experimenting With Christianity*. Some would even say they were agnostics, but they really enjoyed the openness of this fellowship, the music, and the pastor's essays.

Last Stop Christians Sending Postcards from the Edge were dechurched or disillusioned Christians who are in the process of dropping out of organized Christianity. Someone told them about this congregation, and they are giving it a try. Some had their faith rekindled. Others moved on out of Christianity but only after giving the ministry of this congregation an opportunity to change their mind.

Finally, were people *Looking for Faith in All the Wrong Places*. They had tried various religions, then they heard about this congregation. They came to Friday night movies where a member of the congregation—who was a self-professed agnostic—led a lively dialogue about the meaning of various movies for spiritual seekers.

This worked for some people. They made a commitment to Christ and entered the fellowship of this congregation. Often, they did not stay long because they wanted to go deeper into Christianity. They soon realized there was not much depth of faith in this congregation. They wanted more.

Selected Reflections from the Mentoring Group

I began this reflection session by saying, "*Struggling* congregations have an increasing number of spectators when it comes to expectations of continually maturing disciples. There are islands of health and strength, but they do not feel supported by the rest of the congregation. Pastors and staff are weary from trying to push the congregation to be more faithful, effective, and innovative. Willing laypersons are expected to carry a very heavy load of leadership."

"I admit, that is an amazing story!" said Roger. "Who was that well-known pastor? And how did you get connected with that congregation? It does not sound like one with which you would typically consult."

I responded, "Roger, let's leave the actual congregation and its legendary pastor anonymous, as that does not add value to what we can learn from this story. I will say that by the time I consulted with this congregation, they were also a merger of two congregations from sister denominations."

I had known one of the core families for more than 30 years. The congregation decided while their pastor was on a sabbatical, they would invite in a consultant to help them have a sabbatical experience. This family recommended me.

A very positive learning from this case study is that this congregation was willing to try some things to connect with people who are not actively involved in a Christian congregation and were spiritual wanderers. I called them a way station on the edge of Christianity.

By connecting with people who were on the way out of Christian practice, they provided a last hope for a continual influx of people. These people, however, did not stay with this congregation long. They either continued out of Christian practice, or if their Christian commitment was rekindled, they left this congregation to go to one with more people in their age and lifestyle categories. They found places with a more substantial spiritual formation process than this congregation offered.

This congregation did some great things many other congregations might reject, but nothing they did was their silver bullet. Within the next decade this congregation was no more.

The Silver Bullet Plan

Struggling congregations tend to look for unrealistic solutions. I remember watching "The Lone Ranger" television program as a child in the 1950s. It began filming in 1949, and reruns are still on some television stations or streaming services.

The Lone Ranger was committed to truth, justice, and law-abiding people in the American West. The symbol of his focus and strength was not only the mask he wore, but also the silver bullets he used. His silver bullets could bring a quick end to dangerous situations. His goal was not to kill people but to scare them, wound them, or disarm them.

Rarely Living Up to the Hype: The concept of Silver Bullets refers to solutions that are quick, easy, and at times effective. They are touted as the answer to an organization's problems, but they rarely live up to their hype.

Silver Bullets are often based on one-size-fits-all thinking and ignore the unique opportunities and contexts of each organization. They can also create new problems. Silver Bullets do not exist in the real world. Complex problems require complex solutions, and there is no single solution that will work for every situation.

Silver Bullets Are Not the Answer: *Struggling* congregations often want a Silver Bullet—a simple solution that restores them to past glory, or a program or event that will bring instant spiritual revival to the congregation. That is, as long as it does not change the foundational character, nature, and culture of the congregation, plus who is in charge.

Often, the Silver Bullets for which congregations are looking for are things that worked in the past when their situations were different. Silver Bullets are not the answer for congregations. No guaranteed short-term fix will work for congregations that are *Struggling*.

A *Struggling* congregation is smothered by its overly churched culture with an internal focus on making tomorrow a return of yesterday. The direct, dramatic, divine intervention of God is its hope. If God miraculously brought a new vision to the people, they might embrace it.

Ready, Shoot, Aim!

Struggling congregations are not well served by focusing on a Lone Ranger or a Silver Bullet organizational approach. Instead, they need to get ready, shoot, and aim. They get ready by acknowledging they need to try disruptive new and different ways for their congregations to have fresh, vital, and vibrant ministries. This is the toughest step.

They shoot by seeking outside guidance for strategies and ministry practices in which they have or can secure the capacities to implement. This is a humbling step in that they admit they need help.

They aim when trying new and different strategies and

ministry practices and hear the voice of God speaking clearly to them about His focus for their next seasons of ministry. This is the most important step.

Characteristics of Struggling Congregations

Clarity: *Struggling* congregations have not been captivated by God's empowering vision for them for many years—perhaps decades. Their programs, ministries, and activities are plateaued and declining. One or two might be outstanding and thus become that for which they are known. They know their staff and laity fail to provide strong, positive leadership. If God miraculously brought new vision to them, they would embrace it.

Alignment: *Struggling* congregations align their programs, processes, ministries, and activities around what they have always done that brings them at least moderate satisfaction. They believe if they push harder, they may experience a breakthrough.

People: *Struggling* congregations are passive in reaching new people. They respond to those who visit their worship services and programs. Beyond that they are more comfortable with the people who are members, and hesitant about new people who want to change what they do. They cannot understand why younger families with children will not attend and join their congregation.

Faith: *Struggling* congregations have no intentional faith formation efforts. They offer various programs and small groups for people to connect with one another, study, and engage in ministry projects. These are not, however, intentionally for deeper faith formation. When a faith formation effort does arise or is introduced into the congregation, it may bring new, short-term spiritual life to the congregation, but then fades.

Worship: *Struggling* congregations have an established pattern of worship they want to repeat each Sunday. Their challenge is the lack of quality resources they once had to experience this worship. Like other aspects of their congregation, they know they need spiritual renewal, revival, and revitalization. They are just not sure how to achieve that.

Expectations: *Struggling* congregations have an increasing number of spectators when it comes to expectations of continually maturing disciples. There are islands of health and strength, but they do not feel supported by the rest of the congregation. Pastors and staff are weary from trying to push the congregation to be more faithful, effective, and innovative. Willing laypersons are expected to carry a very heavy load of leadership.

Connections: *Struggling* congregations seldom experience new Christians connecting with the congregation from pre-Christian households. An exception may be a child or teenager reached through the congregation's programming. A few people transfer from other congregations. A few have children who become members. More people die or transfer out than connect with the congregation.

Community: *Struggling* congregations have internal community groups who are codependent on one another. As such new people are often not welcome. The member of each community does not realize this, but it is obvious to new people. Unless the new people are assertive in finding community, they will leave within six months to two years after they connect. The internal culture of the congregation is so thick that new people will have trouble understanding it.

Wellbeing: *Struggling* congregations lack unity and have small groups in the congregation who are often in conflict with one another. They may have events and experiences throughout each year that seem to show unity, but just beneath the surface is disruptive to destructive conflict waiting to explode. They may have a group of people who leave the congregation every year or so, or key leaders who decide to quit church or move on to another congregation.

Generosity: *Struggling* congregations face challenges funding their budget each year. They are increasingly dependent on a decreasing number of households who provide a large percentage of their budget receipts. Some of this is due to the aging congregation and the percentage who are conserving their retirement income so as not to outlive their financial resources.

Jackson Street Was Imploding Until It Was in the Middle of a Disaster

"I want an 18-wheeler feeding unit located on the parking lot of Jackson Street Congregation," I declared as the regional disaster response co-coordinator.

"Why?" asked the national coordinator.

"Because it could cause something truly redemptive to happen in a midst of a community significantly impacted by the hurricane."

"I need more than that," replied the national coordinator, "what is the story here?"

The story is that Jackson Street Congregation, which started around the time of World War I in a middle class neighborhood near downtown in a coastal city in the southeast region of the U.S., is now a significantly *Struggling* congregation.

Seven decades resulted in a congregation that peaked following World War II at the capacity of its sanctuary with around 400 in attendance and now has just over 100 in attendance. Their community which started as an all-White middle class community, was now an all-Black lower middle to upper lower class community.

As the pastor said to me, according to his lay leaders, a Black person was only allowed in the building to make a delivery or a repair, and then they had to leave. They could never even think about attending worship or any other activity in the congregation building.

This was not the feeling of the entire congregation nor the pastor and staff, but it was the feeling of the laypersons who controlled the congregation. Particularly one key layperson I call Zachery Taylor. This was not his real name, but his name was that of a former president of the U.S.

Zachery did everything he could to control the congregation so that no innovative or renewing ministry could take place. Only those things the congregation had done for several generations. Besides, the pastor knew better than to preach or teach from any Bible except for the King James Version.

If anyone brought up a new idea, Zachery would shout them down not only in personal or small group conversation, but in public meetings if they persisted. Families he publicly embarrassed typically became quiet, inactive, or left the congregation.

As we moved through a strategic planning process, the idea was voiced of relocating the congregation to the facility of a new congregation that closed about seven miles east of Jackson Street Congregation. This had fairly strong support.

A number of leaders in the congregation realized they had lost the right to minister in this community because of their historic racist attitudes. If they had any hope of a viable future, it would need to be in another place. It would also require them to admit openly their racist attitudes and actions and ask for God's forgiveness for this sin.

You can guess who was opposed to this idea. Zachery and the people who followed him vocally opposed it. Realizing there was growing support for selling the congregation buildings and relocating, they stepped up their opposition.

As part of the process, the congregation held an overnight

retreat away from town. I used an identification process I honed over many years to determine who ought to attend. Zachery was on that list.

The pastor questioned my inclusion of Zachery. He felt Zachery would at some point try to take over the retreat to get his way. I told him I knew that, and I would be ready.

Three choices for the future of the congregation were presented at the retreat. One was selling the building and relocating. When that choice began rising to the top, Zachery stood up from his seat on the front row, turned to the participants and shouted at them this would never happen.

I went and stood inches from Zachery's face, calmly said to him multiple times, "Zachery, you are not going to take over this retreat. Instead, you are going to sit down and be quiet while we allow all the participants to voice their opinions."

Zachery had never had anyone do this to him. He slowly backed away and sat down. His wife came from the back of the room, took him by the arm saying, "Zachery, that is enough. I am taking you home," and they left.

We then took a break. When we came back, we debriefed what had just happened. The remainder of the participants felt a relief, a release, and had a sense they had been rescued.

The remainder of the retreat focused on making plans for the relocation of the congregation. The congregation formally voted a month later with only six negative votes which included Zachery, his wife, and two other couples. These three households soon left the congregation.

Selling the building became the next challenge. It was not difficult. Within a few months they negotiated with a Black congregation to purchase their building. One sense of redemption in the congregation was that this congregation could potentially minister to the community.

In fact, that was one requirement they voiced to the

purchasing congregation. "Would you commit to ministering to this community?" They answered affirmatively.

After the contract was signed, but before the close of the sale, a hurricane came through this coastal city. Jackson Street Congregation and the community around it experienced significant damage. All types of utilities—power, water, etc.—were nonexistent for a couple of weeks.

We were placing feeding units in that whole region to provide food and water for tens of thousands of people. As co-coordinator of the regional command center for my denomination for the next 30 or so days and having the power of suggestion to the national leadership where the feeding units should be stationed, I pressed for one to be in the parking lot of Jackson Street Congregation.

It happened. The impact was great. It was what I hoped would happen.

For the next several weeks, disaster response volunteers, plus people from the Jackson Street Congregation and the Black congregation purchasing their building provided more than 55,000 meals to people in that community.

Once the damage to the Jackson Street building was repaired, and the sale closed, the buying congregation moved in and began worship. They were previously a congregation of 100 to 150 in attendance. During the first service the sanctuary was filled with 450 people. The majority of whom were from the neighborhood around the church building who had been the recipients of the disaster response ministry.

As for Jackson Street Congregation, the church relocated and within a few years were having an attendance three times more than what they had at that their former location. I recall preaching to this vital and vibrant congregation on their second anniversary in their new location.

In the midst of disaster, God broke through and brought redemption.

Selected Reflections from the Mentoring Group

"I have seen this happen so many times. Congregations are able to get church buildings below market value because no one else wants to buy them," said Stewart. "The challenge is that many of these buildings need a lot of repairs, and the ongoing maintenance costs are high. Sometimes it is a good deal for Black congregations to buy buildings from White folks, and sometimes it is not.

"It is for sure the White congregation was never going to reach the Black community as the community knows the reputation of these congregations and will not connect with them no matter how many times they are asked," he said. "They may send their children to various programs and ministries, but that does not bring the parents.

"This was definitely a movement of the Lord. The community needed this church building and a robust congregation in it. God took a disaster and delivered it as manna from heaven!"

Struggling Congregations are Impacted by Things Beyond Their Control

While every collective of congregations is impacted by things beyond their control. *Struggling* congregations are particularly vulnerable. They are already wounded as congregations. External factors and internal factors can push them toward *Spiritless* within a few years.

Here are a view examples:

First, zoning, development, and growth issues can impact congregations. Interstate highways and other major roads can cut through already established housing patterns and place the church facilities on the opposite side of the highway or road from where the target communities or people groups live. This is particularly true of interstate highways with limited access to cross over or under them.

A congregation's community can be zoned for commercial and industrial development which deteriorates the quality and quantity of housing. People relocate in an attempt to save their housing investment before it is too late.

Second, school locations can be an issue. A new school replacing the one in a congregation's immediate context can be built and new families seek to locate near the new school and are no longer in the neighborhoods or communities near the church facilities.

Also, in a lower income community an old school can close. If it was a social and cultural anchor for the neighborhood, then closing the school negatively impacts congregations as another social and cultural anchor.

Third, radical cultural experiences can swiftly shift the character of neighborhoods and community contexts at a pace too fast for congregations to adjust. Extreme examples are a riot, series of demonstrations, or changes in crime patterns in volatile urban areas.

This can cause changes in the demographics in neighborhood and communities so fast that no social, cultural, or religious organization can respond quickly enough to the changes. Many of these changes are typical, inevitable, and possibly should be embraced. The issue here is how fast they happen.

Fourth, deep seated conflict within the congregation about change, staff, doctrine, traditions, and many other things can lead to segments of the congregation leaving and significant diminishing of the leadership and resource base of congregations. The toughest part of this unfortunate conflict in many *Struggling* congregations is that it is the most capable leadership that often leave.

Fifth, severe moral, legal, or financial issues within congregations can disrupt the life and ministry of the congregation within a brief period. These may cause a dimension of conflict with severe trauma from which congregations have difficulty recovering.

Serving Struggling Congregations

An Overview: *Struggling* congregations have a significantly diminished Kingdom impact. The quality of what they do as a Christian community is weakening. Sometimes rapidly or at other times incrementally. They are almost hopelessly stuck as an overly churched culture congregation. The numerical measurement challenges listed for *Stumbling* congregations are now crises for these congregations.

While the word for the transition and change mentioned with *Stumbling* congregations was discontinuous, for *Struggling* congregations the word is disruption. Proactive intervention is needed, yet these congregations often resist it.

Lay leaders who can think and act creatively and innovatively have left these congregations to go to other congregations. The leaders remaining are worthy, committed Christians, but fewer of them have the ability to think and act deeper about the choices ahead of them.

A new journey is needed. Denominations or other outside third parties call what they need revitalization which is a left-brained approach. I believe to get to where these congregations can be embraced by a new journey a deeper spiritual and strategic approach is essential that begins more right brained with initial spiritual steps.

Wise counsel, helpful content, and concerted prayer is needed by *Struggling* congregations.

Counsel: With the theme for *Struggling* congregations of disruptive transition and change, a third party outside the congregation is needed. This can be a consultant, coach, or a denominational staff person with whom they have trust. They need counsel that *business-as-usual* is not working now and will not work in the future.

These congregations need to grant some authority to an outside third party so that some immediate steps can be taken to halt dysfunctional practices. However, trust is essential. It cannot be seized by the outside third party without causing additional harm. It must be freely given so as not to damage the autonomy of the congregation.

Even if the outside person is a trusted individual, emotionally and spiritually the congregational leaders may not be ready to endorse change. If trust is established, and relational contacts with the congregation are regular, they will reach out to the trusted individual or organization at a future time.

It is possible for an intentional interim pastor to play this role once trust is developed with them, or through a covenant agreement before the pastor begins serving in an interim role.

Denominational and parachurch organization plans for helping congregational systems move forward with a new journey in response to God's leadership can be very helpful when congregations are ready. They can be hurtful if the congregation is not ready.

Often resistance to transition and change carries underlying conflict and trauma as mentioned in *Stumbling* congregations. Only here it is more severe and ingrained. Conflict ministry or management may be necessary to create readiness for the new thing God could do in and through these congregations.

Content: In the meantime, until the congregation gets ready, it is important for them to continue serving their membership and hopefully their community context or people groups with a reasonable level of quality ministry. They cannot normally see more than a year in advance. Outside third parties focused on helping them with an annual plan of ministry are beneficial. This outside third-party person or organization needs to bring simple, clear, and attainable ideas for programs, projects, and ministries to help these congregations feel a sense of accomplishment.

Concerted Prayer: *Struggling* congregations as a community of believers are still spiritually seeking. Therefore, a process that engages them in a search for God's direction could bring a breakthrough. I have often used a plan of 100 days of spiritual discernment with congregations with great success in creating readiness for what's next. It engages people in a simple prayer process with two other people which is non-threatening, but very powerful when half or more of the average worship attendance participates.

– 7 –

Spiritless Congregations Cannot Survive Forever

*A **Spiritless** congregation is a remnant group who are so culturally bound they cannot see the new thing God might do through them. The remnant is codependent on their congregational friends, rituals, and facilities. Their goal is to survive one more year. Without a radical new launch or planting they will one day cease to exist. They are fragile. They need the services of a trauma chaplain until there is an open door to confront them with the reality of their situation and the tough choices they must make.*

"Pastor, we never want to hear about this again! You told us about it. We said 'No' so just forget it. Do not ever mention this ridiculous idea again," said an older, long-term lay leader of a **Spiritless** congregation.

"If you want to remain as our pastor, you will carry out our mission to *Reach Everyone for Jesus Christ*. Our last three pastors have failed at this, and we will give you one more chance. It is all up to you."

This pastor, who had earlier in his ministry, served a congregation that closed, did not want this to happen to him again. He was approached by a denominational leader about congregations in this rural and small town county with a similar situation entering into a prayerful dialogue about their future together. Possibly merging into one congregation. He was motivated to do this, yet anxious about a conversation with his leaders.

The denominational leader had met with the pastor search team of this congregation four years earlier. His reaction from that meeting was that there was not a person with any leadership ability among the half-dozen members of this team.

The congregation that once averaged almost 200 in attendance was now down to less than 40 each Sunday. Most were senior adults. Anyone younger was usually related to these senior adults.

A hallway picture gallery of former pastors and staff ministers revealed people well known in the area for the faithfulness and excellence of their ministry in the congregations they went to after serving this congregation.

The pastor search team had already worked for six months and could not agree—or perhaps even find—a pastor who would consider them. A few days after meeting with the team, the denominational leader received a call from the chairperson with a reckless and illegal request.

"If we decide to close the congregation and sell the building, can we divide the money among the membership?"

The response was, "Only if you want to go to jail. In our state when a nonprofit corporation sells its assets, they must be contributed to another nonprofit. No members of the congregation can receive any of the assets. I suspect this law exists everywhere."

Finally, after several more months they connected with their current pastor who was seeking a new congregation. But they continued their same journey with no mission, no vision, no outreach, no evangelism, no disciplemaking, no obvious recognition of the presence of God's Holy Spirit. Thus, *Spiritless*.

Selected Reflections from the Mentoring Group

After telling this story, I turned to the people present in my home and said, "There are many of these congregations. I could fill a book telling story after story of same or similar situations. Likely at least one-fourth of all congregations are in this situation."

"These congregations often have a remnant group of members who are so spiritually myopic they cannot see the new thing God might do in or through them."

"Again," said Stewart, "I have so many of these. It is the same situation I mentioned earlier. I have too many of these in my African American denomination. They are in rural areas, small towns, and cities of all sizes. It may be as many as half of my congregations. The laypeople and the pastors are codependent on one another. They cannot let go and probably should not let go."

"As with *Struggling* congregations, I write a lot of stories about what happens to church facilities once these congregations close," lamented Melissa. "Some are purchased by other congregations. Others are turned into commercial or office businesses. In urban areas too many are torn down to make way for new multi-family housing or commercial developments."

Chad and Thomas both spoke to the issue of getting to these congregations before they close and doing two things. First, asking them if we can nest another congregation—often of a non-English-speaking group—in their facilities. These arrangements help both congregations. Then when the original congregation decides to close, we seek to obtain the building as an incubation center for new congregations or a permanent home for multiple congregations.

Chad spoke with excitement saying, "Oh, I have a story

you must hear! We have a church facility we bought years ago when the original congregation ceased to exist that now houses five congregations in it. They meet at various times during the weekend. There is an Anglo congregation who uses the building and manages it for all the congregations. There are Latino, Korean, Filipino, and Chinese congregations who use the facility. If we have a new congregation who needs space, we squeeze them in until we can find a more permanent location for them."

The custodian for the facility is a red-neck Anglo. He is aways complaining about the foul-smelling food that has clogged the kitchen drain when he comes in on Monday mornings. He usually says it must be the Korean Kimchi.

One Monday he decided he would take the drainpipes under the sink apart and lay the contents out on newspaper, find out who the offending congregation was, and have words with them about the offensive smell.

The only problem was that when he laid the contents out, he found food waste characteristic of all five congregations. This community of congregations, it turns out, was truly a mosaic of the community context.

Too Many Congregations are *Spiritless*

I am not sure which congregation it was that finally led me to call this type of congregation *Spiritless*.

Was it the one that would seat more than 300 and looked like a huge evangelistic crusade tent that had been turned into a cement-block building with two dozen people scattered around the auditorium for worship?

Could it have been the one with half a dozen people huddled in one corner of the fellowship hall, paying a retired pastor to come preach for them each Sunday? They refused many offers for other active congregations to use their sanctuary because they were not their kind of people.

Their former pastor left after he had successfully led the congregation to reach people who lived in the neighborhood around the church facilities. These were a diversity of people racially and ethnically. One weekend when the pastor was away on a missions trip a lay leader told all these people they were no longer welcome in the congregation, and they never came back.

Perhaps it was the congregation that 50 years ago went from a thriving congregation to a remnant congregation when the pastor's infidelity with multiple women in the congregation was exposed. Men in the congregation with guns went looking for the pastor as he fled from town. A group of two dozen people held on to the facility. They kept the congregation open by allowing a non-English language congregation to pay rent to worship there.

Could it have been the congregation where a covocational pastor who worked part-time in three jobs to make a living and could not afford to lose the small stipend from his congregation? They were willing to close but he manipulated them to being codependent on his presence.

Another possibility is a congregation with a good worship center but could not afford to pay for heating it. They were located in a neighborhood of diverse people groups who needed a Christian witness. Their bylaws as a nonprofit in their state called for a certain number of people to form a quorum to make annual legal and financial decisions. They did not have that many members remaining.

If anyone pressed the point, they were no longer a legal corporation, could not appropriately operate, and the charitable donations of the remaining people were no longer tax deductible yet were claimed annually on their taxes.

Is it the dozen or so people I kept meeting and praying

with, who wanted help but would not consider any choices I offered. None of them were younger than 70 years old. They kept wanting to know if there were another congregation who would come join with them at their location so they could have a larger congregation.

What about the congregation with less than 20 in average worship attendance, all senior adults and mostly women, who have an $8 million endowment, and one of the largest organs in North America. They continue to worship and have a full-time pastor. Other than the congregation's attendees getting together for fellowship, their only events are the quarterly public organ recitals.

For most, if not all, of these congregations something radical and even miraculous must happen or they will in the long-term die.

What's worse is collectively throughout North America these congregations have billions of dollars of real estate whose value would be enough to fund the transformation of the Christian witness throughout our continent. Not that I want them to die. I just want their resources to be put to work for the Kingdom.

All I know is that their name is Legion, for there are many. They are also *Spiritless*. Yet the people who are part of these congregations are persons of worth created in the image of God to live and to love.

What is a *Spiritless* Congregation?

For review, a *Spiritless* congregation is a remnant group of members who are so spiritually myopic that they cannot see the new thing God might do in or through them. There are possibilities in their community context and some ministry value in their church buildings.

They have a codependency with their congregation friends and a love for traditions and their church buildings. Their annual goal is to survive one more year.

If they were struck by God's "Triple-D"—the direct, divine, dramatic intervention of God—they might not recognize it. Remember, they are *Spiritless*.

They will not take the risk to do something new because it might further weaken them.

Approach them about merging with another congregation, and they might consider it if the congregation merging with them will come to their location and allow the existing leaders to still control the congregation.

Ask them about another congregation meeting in their building. They might respond, "If they work around the worship schedule of our congregation, we will consider it." They will also be concerned about how the other congregation might treat their building.

Selling their buildings or closing is out of the question for these congregations. If the buildings were significantly damaged by fire, wind or rain, they might consider it. Or if there were a breakdown of major systems like heating, water, or electricity and they did not have the money to make repairs, they could change their minds.

Spiritless congregations have forgotten how to reach new people. Evangelism to them is reactivating inactive members, not reaching new members, much less new Christians. It is possible the remnant group remaining may not have ever been active in new member recruitment or evangelism ministry.

Capable, innovative, missional lay leaders may have long ago moved on from these congregations. The leadership capacities of remaining leaders are often mediocre at best.

Solutions?

First, love the people of these congregations. Get to know them. Affirm them. Listen to their personal stories and the history of their congregations. Pray with them and for them. Develop a deep trust relationship.

Second, invite people from other congregations in the area to get to know them. Offer to provide leaders for special events in these congregations. Pray with them and for them. Be family to them, which should be a characteristic of any network of congregations.

Third, support the pastors of these congregations. Be intentional about including these pastors in fellowship, inspiration, and learning experiences within your network.

Especially provide learning experiences on the choices available for the future of *Spiritless* congregations.

Fourth, include the pastor and lay leaders from these congregations in gatherings that involve the pastors and lay leaders of other *Spiritless* congregations who may be dealing with some of the same challenges. Share at these gatherings stories of *Spiritless* congregations who have transformed.

Fifth, when a *Spiritless* congregation is between pastors, engage them in a conversation about an intentional interim pastor who is trained and experienced in helping *Spiritless* congregation consider their choices at this stage of life.

Sixth, do not hesitate to offer solutions to them as you deepen your relationship with them. You never know when God has been able to break through to them and they are open for something radical to happen such as launching as a new congregation with the assistance of their denomination or a church planting network.

Seventh, launch a new congregation in this location, if possible, in the facilities of the *Spiritless* congregation. The remnant group eventually can be a participating part of the new congregation. The remnant group should not have any significant leadership role at first, however, so the old culture does not infect the new culture.

What Are the Characteristics of a Spiritless Congregation?

Clarity: *Spiritless* congregations are focused on survival. They would not recognize nor respond to a new vision from God. They will not take the risk to do something new because it might further weaken them. They are so culturally bound that only through radical outside effort that mandates them to change will they be able to find a way forward.

Alignment: In *Spiritless* congregations, the concept of alignment has no meaning. They are just trying to keep their programs, processes, ministries, and activities alive. They may do this even if they have no one to lead them. The only hint of alignment is that anything they can still do is aligned with the goal of survival.

People: *Spiritless* congregations have forgotten how to reach new people and realize they may not have much to offer them if they came. Also, if new people do come, their motive for receiving them is so the new people will extend the life of the congregation. Thus, not to serve the new people but for new people to serve the old people.

Faith: *Spiritless* congregations go through the motions of faith formation. They have some of the right programs they are engaged in out of tradition and habit, rather than out of fresh, effective approaches to develop a deep faith journey for congregants. A few people have deep spiritual lives, but either have no life energy to apply what is in their heart or are burned out from doing so.

Worship: *Spiritless* congregations also go through the motions of worship as they have traditionally experienced it. Worship must be faithful to the way they have engaged in worship for many years. Worship is a remembrance of how they culturally seek to praise and worship our Triune God every week. For a portion of the congregation, it is about going through the motions every week.

Expectations: *Spiritless* congregations have pastors and staff who easily burnout trying to get the congregation to move forward. Their pastor has burned out trying to get the congregation moving forward, has given in and seeks a new congregation to move to, or is coasting to retirement. Lay leaders try to keep the congregation active for the sake of aging parents, their adult children who are hanging on, and their grandchildren who need the congregation.

Connections: *Spiritless* congregations have people transferring out of the congregation or dying. Few new people connect with the congregation. They count success as no one leaving who is a significant financial contributor to the congregation. They may even wish that a nearby congregation would merge in with them and provide them with new connections.

Community: *Spiritless* congregations hold close the community of people they have related to for many years. They get jealous if new people connect with their community. A few people with a gracious spirit will welcome the new people into a deep community relationship. The remainder will not get close to them as their co-dependence on their remaining friends is deep.

Wellbeing: *Spiritless* congregations are dysfunctional systems. The remnant leadership have stories of various periods where unity was illusive for many years. There are congregational secrets about pastors and staff persons who had to leave for various reasons. The remaining leadership are just trying to hold things together and hoping tomorrow a miraculous renewal will take place.

Generosity: *Spiritless* congregations have similar generosity challenges as do **Struggling** congregations. The pool of people from whom they can draw budget support is smaller each year. Deferred maintenance and major building systems replacement are beyond their reach. They have already closed down part of their building, but they are committed to hanging on as long as possible.

A *Spiritless* Congregation Experiences a Fiery Revolution

Sometimes only a revolution will save a dying congregation.

The revolution began when Martin Kaiser declared martial law at Castle Heights First Church. He suspended the bylaws and took charge. No one stopped him. The revolution lasted for two years in this congregation located in the rural-urban fringe of a mid-sized metropolitan area.

Martin began serving as the interim pastor of Castle Heights First Church as summer transitioned into fall. On a typical Sunday, about 40 people attended a worship center designed for more than 375 people.

Once filled with worshippers, Castle Heights engaged in decades of what were caricatured as *Attendance-Reduction Campaigns*. They simply could not get along with one another and continued to drive attendees away, which discouraged new people from connecting with them.

The story of the congregation's business meeting when people threw hymns across the worship center at one another still circulate in the community. Within the congregation are denials the episode ever happened.

Their journey included a series of short-term pastors.

Once the honeymoon phase for each pastor ended, they were no longer welcome. They each did something that offended a family of long-term members, and that was enough to get them fired.

Martin knew he must change the spiritual culture of this congregation, or they would continue to be repeat offenders. He began preaching, teaching, and trying to lead them to unfreeze from their current place in congregational ministry, and to go on a new Kingdom adventure.

For the first four months, they ignored him. Perhaps he would go away, too.

The congregation was run by five deacons—decent men, but untrained in the responsibilities of a New Testament deacon. They certainly were not the kind found in Acts of the Apostles chapter six. Instead, they resembled the high priests and Sanhedrin from the Gospels.

These deacons and the congregation were *Spiritless*. This was a dying and overly churched culture congregation. They were directionless, not into disciplemaking—much less studying about true discipleship. Basic Bible lessons from familiar stories and passages were enough for them.

But the preacher better be careful. None of this Sermon on the Mount liberal heresy—particularly not the Beatitudes. Even with this attitude they survived by continuing to call the next pastor. Discouraging each new pastor so he would leave after a few years seemed to be their unconscious goal.

Smoldering Embers: The day after Christmas during Martin's first year, their church facilities caught fire, destroying all their primary buildings. Firefighters fought the flames with great courage, but the buildings could not be saved due to the fire being too advanced before enough equipment and personnel arrived on-site.

The following Sunday, the remaining congregation gathered at a nearby school gymnasium. During the initial part of the worship service, people shared their thoughts about what the now-demolished buildings meant to them, particularly the memorable events that took place in the church facilities. Weddings, funerals, baptisms, music and drama programs, moments of personal spiritual awakening all were mentioned.

Interim pastor Martin declared, "Our congregation did not burn. Our buildings burned. You are the people of God at Castle Heights. You are very much alive. God will lead us forward. From these smoldering embers, God will do a new thing!"

He preached from Isaiah 43:19, which says, "Be alert, be present. I'm about to do something brand-new. It's bursting out! Don't you see it?"

Knowing the dysfunctional nature of the congregation and understanding that radical action was necessary, Martin then declared martial law. By now they began to trust him and followed his lead.

From that point on, Martin could now effectively serve as an intentional interim pastor for them focusing on planting a new congregation from the smoldering embers. The congregation still viewed themselves as buildings, while he championed the idea of the congregation as people in a spiritual relationship with God.

The congregation not only lost its buildings but also had recently paid staff salaries from its financial reserves. They were close to being out of money.

Spiritual Challenges: In January, Martin preached a message about stewardship and tithing as an act of obedience to God. He challenged everyone who had never tithed ten percent of their income through the congregation to do so during the month of February.

During February, offerings increased significantly, and they were even higher in March. People noticed the difference it made, and many followed in obedience, which gave them the confidence to continue.

The spring brought forth a sermon series on "Out of the Ashes: Lessons God Teaches Us from the Fire." Attendance gradually began to increase, reaching 75 or more by Easter.

As congregation attendance had declined in recent years, programming decreased to almost nothing. Martin decided he needed to start a disciplemaking process among the active congregation. He suggested initiating small groups. Leaders indicated this had been tried before and did not work. They were not interested.

Martin was not discouraged. He and his wife invited 12 people to their home for a weekly dinner and to study a book together on spiritual renewal. These people were then challenged to form their own group and teach the same book.

The number of people involved in this process grew from the original 12 to nearly 75, which is almost double the number of adults who attended worship before the fire. Weekly sermons on spiritual growth supported the small groups.

Benchmarks: The fire chief, who led the crews fighting the church fire, plus his wife, began attending Castle Heights. He said he was inspired by their story to come but was initially afraid. "I was afraid to come because I could not save the church buildings and wondered if people would blame me for the destruction."

"No, you are not to blame. I do not hear anyone suggesting that," responded Martin.

Having the fire chief as part of the congregation symbolized healing and affirmed the congregation consists of people, not buildings.

The deacons were an important benchmark. By default, they had served as the congregation's managers for many years as the committee structure faded away. They were challenged to transition from management to engaging in the work of ministry.

As the fellowship of the congregation and the ministry of the deacons became active, attendance at the congregation exceeded 100. It had been many years since this number of people had worshiped at Castle Heights on a weekly basis.

Even with all the progress, Martin felt things were still moving too slow. He took the risk of assuming even more authority to see if the congregation would continue to follow his lead. Many things needed to happen quickly to get the congregation into a new building and thriving as a new congregation.

He appointed a layperson who had the expertise and willingness to oversee the removal of the debris left by the fire. The debris was a constant reminder of what had happened. A cleared lot ready for a new building would symbolize a promise of the future.

A former member with building expertise returned to the congregation during this time, bringing the experience and wisdom needed for a new church building. With these two people as the foundation, he recommended a building committee to the congregation.

The building project was started. They moved into the new facility two years after the fire, with no debt incurred between their insurance benefits and the funds given or raised. Before they moved into the new building, they were already averaging close to 200 attendees.

The new facility was smaller than the previous one, accommodating less than 300 worshippers. The total square footage of the new building was 24,000, down from 35,000. On the first Sunday in the new building, they filled it to capacity.

The sermon focused on Moses standing before the burning bush that was not consumed. While the church building had burned, the congregation remained unharmed. They received a mandate from the fire for their future.

Leadership: As Castle Heights began anew, they secured a part-time children's minister and a part-time youth minister.

This offered essential program support for the families they were serving. Additionally, they hired a part-time business administrator.

A new type of volunteer leadership role was established after the church bylaws were rewritten. A 12-member leadership council was formed consisting of the pastor, church administrator, worship pastor, six individuals with specific program and ministry assignments, and three at-large representatives from the congregation. The pastor chairs this group.

This formalized the deacon's role as no longer managing but ministering to the membership and community. After almost a decade, the deacons could serve as deacons again.

Four months after the congregation moved into the new building, they voted to call a new pastor. Since his arrival, worship attendance is already averaging more than 250. A second worship service is now being considered.

New suburban development is preparing to arrive in this congregation's community. Within a five-mile radius of their location, 2,000 homes are projected to be built. It remains unknown whether this congregation will be able to connect with the new residents. The next chapter of their story has yet to be written.

They are no longer *Spiritless*. It will take another three to five years to evaluate the changes and determine their position within the collective of congregations.

Selected Reflections from the Mentoring Group

"George, I caught you!" Becky almost shouted. "When you talked about *Struggling* congregations you said something about an outside person forcing congregations to do something that did violence to their autonomy. Here in the Castle Heights story, you endorsed the interim pastor declaring martial law. I think we deserve an explanation!"

"Thank you, Becky. I really did expect that challenge and would have been disappointed if I did not get it from someone," I said, chuckling as I spoke. I went on to explain.

This is an application to congregations of what is commonly called the *aging parent syndrome*. While this is not a formally recognized medical or psychological diagnosis, it does describe the common challenges that arise when roles shift, and adult children are caring for their aging parents.

Spiritless, old age congregations must have caring outside third parties who willingly speak into their situation and are prepared to take radical action to save these congregations from themselves. People with less than genuine motives seek to takeover these congregations. Kingdom resources owned by these congregations are lost. The people of the congregations are being abused spiritually and emotionally through multiple dimensions of codependency.

Someone or some entity must be willing to take decisive action for the good of the people in these congregations, and the overall good of the witness of the Christian Church. However, it is a tricky situation. Local congregational and denominational polity are at play. Legal issues abound.

Like the adult child who takes decisive action for the care and wellbeing of a parent who is resistant and fights certain actions, whomever intervenes in these situations needs to be prepared for ugly responses to their actions.

In the session on **Struggling** congregations, I talked about the action I took with Jackson Street against Zachery Taylor. This was not an action against the congregation which would have been wrong at that point. It was an action against one bully. I knew it was a risk. No one else knew I was going to do this. It could have turned out bad. But it did not.

I cannot tell you how long I prayed about this before coming to the retreat prepared to do it.

I would not have done this with a congregation at that point. I have threatened legal actions against congregations who were *Spiritless*, but I never took these actions. I spoke to them this way to help them see the hopelessness of their situation.

I have cried with congregations in dialogue with them over their inaction once they became *Spiritless*. No easy answers exist.

Serving Spiritless Congregations

If discontinuous was the description of the transition and change needed by *Stumbling* congregations, and disruption for *Struggling* congregations, what is the word for Spiritless congregations?

It is destruction. A harsh word for sure. But the right word.

It means that what was now needs to end. What could become needs to be launched. It is about a totally new venture in this place, among the people in the context or the people groups in the area.

The current mainstream word for this is replant. To let the context or people groups guide what needs to happen next for the work of God's Kingdom to abound. The old must end. The new must rise.

In a totally new venture, nothing which was part of the old can be part of the new. At times this includes the church facilities. It is like entering a new missions field where the Christian witness has not previously been present. It starts with understanding the context and the people groups and what type of Christian witness might be effective.

Three words characterize this approach: Conversion, Compassion, and Commission.

Conversion: The form of Christian witness and congregation currently in existence needs to morph to a new form. It needs to be a new congregation—one which does not have the cultural and spiritual baggage of the old. Bless what was and celebrate what is becoming. It speaks to the image of not being able to put new wine into old wine skins in Luke 5:37-39.

This must be initiated from outside the dying congregation. Participants in the waning congregation can serve in supporting roles but cannot be part of the key or core leadership for the first three years to empower a totally new culture.

The conversion must be complete.

Compassion: A new dimension of compassion and empathy must be expressed for the households, community, and people groups who are the focus of the new ministry. In some situations, the context is aware of the former congregation, so the new congregation must show a deep, refreshing, and loving character in their relationship to the community and people God calls them to serve.

Love first. Offer relational and spiritual conversation. Engage in compassionate ministry. Enlist for the new congregation when the timing is right.

Why this order? To hardwire into the culture of the new congregation Kingdom growth rather than church growth.

Commission: A new understanding of the Great Commission in the spirit of the Great Commandment must permeate the commitment of the leaders and core group who launch a new congregation.

They should use a missiological approach to understand the context, community, and people groups. How can they present the gospel message to people in a way that transforms the context and people groups miraculously to be more Christ-like individually and collectively.

This self-sacrificing approach is one where we celebrate the reality that God gives the increase.

It is counter-intuitive to many denominational and para-church strategies for launching new congregations, but it is what our world needs today. Too many denominational and parachurch strategies are about church growth rather than Kingdom growth.

– 8 –

The Difference Maker for Congregations

What I Want You to *Know* About Difference Making

With all the concepts, phrases, and titles in this book, along with the five collectives, ten characteristics for each collective, and the congregational case studies, is it time to succinctly describe a congregation which is soaring with faith?

The great challenge is that no absolute, left-brained, logical, boxed answer exists. All answers are imperfect, right-brained, feelings-based, and centered rather than boxed. It is a situation where you will know it when you experience it. The answer will always be subjective and not objective. At best it depends on the congregation, its context, or the people groups by whom it is seeking to be received.

Now that we have arrived at the concluding chapter, I want to give soaring-with-faith congregations a clearer title. I call them *FaithSoaring Congregations*. This moniker comes with a warning. Do not allow it to become a trite term embraced by a large group of congregations. It is intended to be farther up and farther in, beyond the horizon, over the next mountain range, or somewhere out there. It applies to no more than 10 percent of all congregations. The exact number is an allusive target.

If it becomes commonplace and you apply it to legions of

congregations, it will lose its meaning. We must always see it as the leading edge of congregational life—always teaching, pulling, and inspiring us to greater potential in God's Kingdom. The leading edge is always a moving target.

A congregation with *FaithSoaring* character and nature today may no longer be *FaithSoaring* five to seven years from now, when the next pandemic interrupts the journey of congregations, or some crisis internally impacts the congregation. Other congregations who catch a wave of innovation may soar past them, travel through a cosmic wormhole, or morph into a new understanding of congregational life.

I do have heartbreaking news. Your congregation can have high quality clarity, alignment, people, faith, worship, expectations, connections, community, wellbeing, and generosity, and still not be *FaithSoaring*. *FaithSoaring* is not a completed checklist that takes you where God was intending for you to go. It is so much more than a left-brained inventory.

Even more than the continuum shared in the section on *A Debate Broke Out*.

FaithSoaring Congregations understand soaring with faith. They cannot always describe it to you, but they get it. They may be able to reflect on how they got there, and they will likely tell you it was not how they planned to get there.

Curves and elevation changes characterized their journey. Interruptions happened. New innovations arose that were not predictable yet enriched their journey.

It is not always helpful or true for a congregation to declare they are *FaithSoaring*. It is more dependable for people outside a congregation who have experienced multiple *FaithSoaring Congregations* to make that declaration. If a congregation declares itself *FaithSoaring* they may believe they have arrived and stop innovating. This would be terrible news.

I was part of a staff where this happened. The leader cast a vision for a future of soaring with faith. We implemented a strategy to fulfill the vision. Within a few years obvious progress ensued. Then the leader experienced incredibly wise mentors telling him that under his leadership the needed transformation had taken place.

Once he received that affirmation, he declared his personal perspective on leading an exceptional ministry organization was affirmed by international leaders. Immediately thereafter innovation began waning until it ceased.

Ultimately, what I want you to know is that a congregation which is soaring with faith cannot be convincingly defined. It must be experienced. And it is fleeting. It can disappear.

What I Want You to *Feel* About Difference Making

I want you to feel and experience the difference between a congregation working so hard to be *Soaring* but missing it. Consider one which is like a highly engineered electric car that is sailing along the autobahn in Germany propelled forward by a driverless guidance system toward the destination to which God is pulling it.

I want you to feel the pull of the cloud by day and the fire by night which provides obvious signs for your spiritual and strategic congregational journey. I want you to show amazement at the beauty of a mighty cloud moving across the horizon before you, and the passion of the red hot fire that guides your congregation through the challenges of the night by clearly lighting your way.

The cloud and the fire represent the navigation of your congregation's journey during both times of light and darkness as the journey is never fully calm and still moves forward.

I want you to meet Jesus in Galilee where he has gone before you as our Triune God always does. I want you to experience the resurrected Lord in ways you did not expect. I want your congregation to be more than one which has all ten characteristics, but one that feels the exhilaration of God going before you as your eternal leader.

I want you to feel the warmth that comes over you when you are possessed by the assurance your congregation is in the center of God's will. This assurance can allow you to discern the new thing God is doing in and through your life and the life of the whole congregation. This assurance can also guide you in times when the sinful actions of humanity distract you and take you momentarily away from the focus God has given your congregation.

FaithSoaring will always be a captivating experience to the extent the feeling you are on the right journey will be both challenged and affirmed. Listen to the tests and the affirmations. The challenges may allow you to sharpen the focus of your journey. The affirmations may be the strength you need in times of challenge, weariness, and outrunning your leadership supply lines that the journey is still sure and true.

One more thing.

I am big—and not all people are—on the spiritual call of God on the lives of people individually and collectively. I want you to feel and experience the joy and peace only possible when an ever-increasing number of disciples in your congregation serve with clarity about the call of God on their lives. Rather than just falling in line with what leaders tell you.

What I Want You to *Do* About Difference Making

I want you to challenge your congregation to be *FaithSoaring*. If your congregation is on a spiritual and strategic journey to become a *FaithSoaring* congregation, consider these challenges.

Challenge One is to gather insights from congregational staff, lay leaders, and active followers. Ask them for evidence the ten characteristics are present and impacting the spiritual and strategic journey of the congregation. Ask them about the overall spiritual and strategic evidence your congregation is *soaring with faith.*

Challenge Two is to ask wise outside mentors if your congregation is *soaring with faith.* But do not ask them only by telling them your story. Invite them to come to your congregation and experience a typical weekend. Allow them to talk with anyone they want to about the *FaithSoaring* characteristics of your congregation.

In debriefing them, question them about what they saw, felt, smelled, heard, and tasted in and around your congregation during the weekend. Ask them about the presence of positive, spiritual passion concerning the future of the congregation toward which God is pulling it. Invite them to share evidence they experienced of *FaithSoaring* or the lack thereof.

Challenge Three is to look for evidence that spiritual, lifestyle, and cultural transformation is happening. Seek testimonies from people in the community context or among the people groups God asks your congregation to serve. Remember that *Soaring* congregations are more about Kingdom growth than church growth. Discover evidence that the context or people groups you serve are increasingly more Christ-like and loving plus continually experiencing spiritual transformation because of your ministry.

Without this evidence you may only be a *Strong* congregation. And also remember you cannot go into the context and people groups and declare you are *Soaring.* The people in the context or within the people groups must present you with evidence of this by the testimonies of their own lives and ministries.

Challenge Four is to conduct a teaching congregation event where you invite other congregations to visit you for several days—including a weekend—and learn how you are *soaring with faith.* The best part of doing this is not necessarily the event. The best part is putting together how you would describe what has happened in the life and ministry of your congregation over the past five to seven years that makes you a *FaithSoaring Congregation.*

You must put your principles and practices into writing and explain to others what God is doing in and through your congregation. Only then can you truly realize the depth and breadth of God's leading in your congregation over multiple years.

A teaching congregation event will have as many stories of lives spiritually transformed as it will talk about the processes of transition and change over multiple years. It must show the congregation who you were, the one you became, and the one you will continue to become. Always remember your situation is unique.

Many years ago, a regional denominational organization invited senior pastor Bill Hybels and the Willow Creek Community Church worship team to lead a model seeker worship experience for leaders throughout their region. Following an evening of worship, the next day the Willow Creek leaders conducted workshops on various aspects of their approach.

One common refrain in each workshop was, "Don't go home and try to replicate what you saw last night. Learn the principles and framework of what you saw and decide how it might work in your situation. Why? Because your situation is unique."

Challenge Five comes out of a realization that the journey is not over yet. God is not finished with your congregation. There are more mountains to climb. Five to seven years into your *FaithSoaring Congregation* journey, begin asking God to reveal to you the places farther up and farther in His Kingdom where He is leading you.

Years ago, I led a congregational retreat in a mountain location. We took one afternoon off for recreation. A group of us decided we would climb the mountain right behind the retreat center. We were told it was a 90-minute climb and there was an easy trail to follow.

We began the climb. About a third of the way up we saw an obvious rest and lookout point used by others who had come before us. We surveyed the view and realized how different the perspective was from such a short climb. We saw things about the retreat center we would have never known without making this climb. For one we saw how close it was to the nearby town even though the crooked road to get to the center had taken 20 minutes or more.

Further, we had a distinct perspective on the range of mountains around us. We could see farther up and farther into the range. We observed where light and shadows created by the clouds above revealed the beauty of God's creation.

At a second rest area we had a similar experience. Fresh vistas. New beauty. More "Wow."

We then reached the summit of the mountain. At that point, a new even more beautiful view was before us. I said, "Wow, this is wonderful and was worth the climb." Another person exclaimed, "Whoa, I would never have believed it if someone just told me about it and I had not made the climb."

We could see for miles and miles. The mountain before us exploded with beauty. We could see so far off into the distance that it almost seemed like the mountains joined the clouds.

As we made our way down the mountain to the retreat center, we debriefed our experience. It fit in with our retreat agenda about the journey of congregations. Among the insights offered by our small group of hikers were these:

- If you are unwilling to go on a journey, you will never know what is out there. You would miss the wonderful things God has prepared for you.
- Your journey will give you a new perspective. You will discover new things you could not see at the beginning of your journey.

- You can look back and see the progress you are making while also looking forward to seeing the challenges you face.

- You will discover new things, new opportunities, new blessings, new resources that you would never have known.

- Discovery of your place in the collection of congregations—just as each mountain has a story to tell—will help you see your uniqueness.

- Our climb of 90 minutes was up a mountain that was a smaller one in the range. By making the journey we could see there were many other mountains to climb. In the same way, soaring with faith takes us up one mountain, and gives us a vision of other opportunities in God's Kingdom. Our climb may be just the first journey of soaring with faith. God has more journeys for us than we can image.

What I Want You to **Become** in Difference Making

It is not that I want your congregation to become a *Faith-Soaring Congregation*. It is more that I want you to live into God's full Kingdom potential for your congregation. If in the process, you soar with faith then you are indeed a *FaithSoaring Congregation* for at least a season of your life.

I have a declaration and a confession for you.

I am simultaneously transfixed by my greatest strength and my greatest weakness about helping congregations soar with faith to reach their full Kingdom potential. My strength is a declaration. My weakness is a confession. And they are the same thing.

My declaration and my confession are that I want every congregation to be exactly what it is God is calling them to be at the current time, in the future, and in their unique situation. I do not want them to be what any prognosticator declares they ought to be. Or bestselling book. Or speaker. Or prescriptive process. Or diagnostic tool. Or successful congregation. Or strong-willed pastor. Or me.

I only want them to be exactly what God wants them to be. They are to fulfill the desire of God's heart for them. In that fulfillment is boundless joy and exhilaration.

This declaration is my greatest strength because it affirms the unique call of God for each congregation. It sees every congregation as a community of persons of great worth and value created in the image of God to live and to love.

This confession is also my greatest weakness because it requires a dimension of altruism that alludes more than 90 percent of congregations. It leaves congregations open to less than the best solutions for their future.

Soaring with faith is a learning journey without an end. It does have a beginning. This occurs when a congregation decides it wants to be all God intends for it. When it wants to serve others more than itself with a reckless abandonment for what is safe and secure.

Christianity needs a greater spirit of reckless abandonment.

A perception. Many people do not get it about living as a congregation which soars with faith. In fact, I did not even get it for about two decades myself. It is a learned understanding. And the learning never ceases.

Because I get it now, it is still hard for me to explain what it means to soar with faith to people who are *back seat* or *lower room* people. God calls us to the front seat of the journey and a room with a higher view of His will for us.

Not to the models and language learned in the business, government, or military worlds. They will not fit the spiritual and voluntary association world of a faith-based Christ-centered, spiritual community.

Let me illustrate with just one concept. Disciple. What does it mean to be a Christian disciple? Pick a definition that fits your understanding.

A Christian disciple is a person who ...

1. is a faithful congregational member who regularly attends worship, engages in various Bible-related and theological studies, and increases their knowledge of Christianity and congregation culture.

2. is person who seeks to grow deeper in their faith by Bible study, prayer, giving money to the congregation and other Christian ministries, and participates in various outreach and compassion ministry efforts.

3. seeks to be more like Jesus in their daily life by expressing God's unconditional love to all they encounter, and even proactively advocates for the salvation of all and walking with Jesus as they grow in grace, knowledge, and sacrificial Christ-like service.

4. comes to understand God's call upon their life and endeavors to fulfill that calling with an "all-in" lifestyle of humble service to the people and causes God directs them to so that people might receive Jesus as Savior and Lord and serve Him unconditionally.

It takes all types of disciples to empower a congregation to soar with faith and reach its full Kingdom potential. For this to happen, however, I believe a minimum of one-fourth of the average number of active attending adults present on a typical weekend for worship must be of up to the fourth type stated above.

I was coaching a congregation once where a younger leader suggested we should not use the word "disciple" because too many people do not know what that is or what it means.

That suggestion was agony for me. This is a core concept of

Christianity, as we are called to be followers of Jesus. We are to be students of Christ-like life. We are to be disciples who make disciples.

What I Want You to *Fulfill* About Difference Making

Often a program or project approach involving seeking success by pushing forward does not produce sustainable significance for congregations. One summer during college I served as an interim music and youth director for a congregation.

This was early enough in my ministry that I was trying to figure out what worked best to empower the life journey of teenagers. I was still a teenager myself. I was only a year older than the oldest students. The best I knew to do was to replicate the programs and projects I had learned growing up in various congregations.

It was an activity-based summer, maybe too many activities, according to feedback from exhausted parents and chaperons.

As one of the parents and I were sitting around evaluating the summer, he expressed appreciation for all I had done with the teenagers in the congregation and community. He acknowledged it had been a remarkably busy summer, but a great one for his teenagers who had really connected with the congregation at a deeper dimension than ever before.

It had been overwhelming for his wife, Brenda, who broke down crying during our mountain retreat one evening saying the summer had been so busy her family had not been able to take their vacation. She was sufficiently distraught that her husband, Daniel, came the next day to take her back home.

I did not know at the time that part of her emotional response related to families in the congregation who were talking about leaving the congregation to form a new congregation with a different focus.

In the evaluation with Daniel, he raised the issue of progress. Brenda and Daniel helped chaperon many youth events while their children were teenagers. Daniel's concern was that his children were getting increasingly involved in the congregation. This was good. But he did not see they were making spiritual progress. They were busy and involved, but maturing in their faith and forming spiritually alluded them. He and Brenda did not know how to guide their teenagers to move more deeply spiritually.

Then he asked me how I as someone going into Christian ministry manage the issue. "You teach and serve as an example for teenagers about Jesus and congregational life, but they just do not seem to experience visible progress in their faith and lifestyle," he said.

The feeling of fright rushed through my veins. My blood pressure surely shot up at that moment. The emotion of flight— getting out of this conversation—came over me. All I could say was, "I have not figured that out yet. I am only 19 myself."

Even at that youthful age I was good at *doing church*. But I had not yet figured out how to help people *be the Church* which God sent Jesus to die for.

This is not unlike Christians who are faithful to a church community. We understand the programs, ministries, and activities of congregational life. We are still trying to figure out the process or spiritual journey aspects of the Christian life, much less how to be pulled forward by our Triune God to soar with faith.

I want you and your congregation to know, feel, do, become, and fulfill all to which God is calling you. If that results in you becoming a *FaithSoaring Congregation*, I will rejoice with you. Let me hear from you. I want to know your story.

The Seven Keys to Full Surrender to God as a *FaithSoaring Congregation*

FaithSoaring Congregations are not successful congregations. They are not congregations doing something significant that causes them to stand out among the more than 400,000 congregations in North America. They are congregations who have fully surrendered to God's leadership.

Way too often it is declared that the key to *soaring with faith* is to have the right pastor. This approach embraces an only partially correct concept that everything rises and fall on one leader. It is leadership rather the leader.

It is said that successful pastors lead successful congregations. Pastors with significant abilities lead significant congregations who serve as models for other congregations. I say pastors who are fully surrendered to the *Missio Dei*—the mission of God—lead congregations who are fully surrendered to God's will for them.

However, the pastor is only one of seven keys to a *FaithSoaring Congregation* fully surrendered to God's will. When I began consulting with congregations in the mid-1970s my denomination had a major emphasis on the lead pastor and saw this person of the one and only key. I rejected this from the beginning of my consultation ministry.

I have said throughout my ministry there are five to seven keys to a fully surrendered congregation who might be seen as a *FaithSoaring Congregation*. Fifty years ago, I saw the number as five. Since then, God has shown me two more which I added to the list.

Test your congregation against these seven if you believe you are a *FaithSoaring Congregation*, or if you believe God wants you to be *FaithSoaring*?

First—Pastor: The lead pastor is the first of seven keys to a fully surrendered *FaithSoaring Congregation*. A spiritual call to pastoral ministry, life strengths applicable to exceptional Christian ministry, and a personality that loves people and wants the very best for them as Christian disciples are among the essential characteristics needed in these pastors.

Second—Leaders: There is no way the pastor can do it alone. No way staff and lay leaders can simply count on the lead pastor to shoulder the burden alone. Multiple leaders must accept God's challenge to the ministry of leadership with the pastor as an initiating and respected leader. As stated above, one-fourth of active, attending laypersons present on a typical Sunday for worship must understand God's call in their lives, and have an "all in" Christ-like lifestyle effectively practiced through their congregation.

It is these people representing up to one-fourth of the active congregation who must be captured by God's empowering vision and have great clarity and alignment surrounding this vision.

Third—Clarity: Clarity concerning God's empowering vision for the congregation must captivate the spiritual lives of not only the lead pastor, staff, and key lay leaders. It must permeate the entire active congregation. A clear understanding that is continually renewed of where the congregation is headed under God's Kingdom-focused leadership must be present.

Fourth—Alignment: Alignment of everything the congregation does with the clarity of God's empowering vision must be a major emphasis. Many good things can be done, but only when we discover that which is worthy, and focus on how it aligns with the clarity God has given the congregation, will there be success, significance, and surrender to a ministry of soaring with faith.

Fifth—Disciplemaking: Help all who resolve to do so to willingly engage in a sacrificial, surrender, and "all-in" disciplemaking journey to become fully devoted followers of Christ. To come to an understanding of God's call on their lives. To be deployed in service within the congregation, community context, and among people groups that God's world might be spiritually transformed.

In this regard, more Marys than Marthas will be needed. The Marys will desire to serve and touch with God's love the lives of people through high-touch, effective ministry. Marthas will want to keep the systems of the congregation functioning with efficiency and with the high-tech needed.

Pause for a minute and recall what Jesus said in Luke 10:42: "Here is only one thing worth being concerned about. Mary has discovered it, and it will not be taken away from her." (New Living Translation)

Sixth—Resources: Finances, materials, and facilities are absolutely essential. Internally these empower pastors, staff, and laypersons who are fully committed to the journey. These are the people who will also themselves provide at least a tithe and likely go beyond the tithe into the realm of generosity.

Beyond this, the ability to discover and harvest various resources must be part of the ongoing support strategy for *FaithSoaring* congregations. When I was pastor of an inner-city congregation, we called this the scavenger approach to ministry. The resources are out there. We must go find them. At times the resources are not money or commodities. They are expertise and experience various people can bring to a congregational journey.

Seventh—God's Timing: My decades of experience in working with congregations tell me the other six can be present, but the most important key is whether moving forward at a certain time and place is within God's timing for a congregation. The clear empowerment of God for right here and right now must be present.

If moving a congregation to soaring with faith does not happen when it appears everything is in place for it to happen, then we may have misinterpreted God's timing. Something may be lacking we do not see. Something may be getting ready to happen we do not yet understand.

This key alone is enough to make the effort fail for reasons it takes a while for us to understand, if we ever do. I have seen it too many times not to know the reality of this key.

When these seven keys have clarity and alignment then something awesome happens that God has ordained.

Read this Last!

I invite you to come to Greenville, South Carolina, to spend four days with me and a small group of people just like the mentoring groups referred to in this book.

Interested? If so, email me at BullardJournal@gmail.com. In the subject line indicate this is about *The Greenville Hub*. I will respond with details.

Our focus during this time will be on helping congregations become *FaithSoaring*. Plus, to help those who consult with or coach congregations.

I hosted this type of experience from 2015 through 2019, and then the pandemic hit. After I finished helping the almost 100 congregations I served in Columbia, South Carolina, work through the pandemic, I retired to Greenville, South Carolina, in 2022.

Now I am ready to restart these dialogue groups focused on this book and the five collectives to which it refers.

Two things will be different about these dialogue groups compared to the previous round of dialogues.

First, I am doing these in partnership with a wonderfully experienced coach and teacher whose focus is first impressions, guest services, and cultivating volunteers in congregations.

Second, experiences will typically be from Friday afternoon through Monday afternoon, which will allow opportunities for you to visit selected congregations in the Greenville area and then debrief the experience.

If you simply want to keep up with what I am writing, connect with one of my blogs on Substack. ForthTelling Innovation, my primary ministry connection blog, is at https://forthtelling innovation.substack.com/.

George Bullard's Journal is where I write more personal things and is more focused on my Baptist background. It can be found at https://georgebullard.substack.com/.

I also write regular columns for The Baptist Paper on the work and ministry of the local denominational organization in Baptist life known as the Baptist association. I focus on how it can serve as a family of congregations in fellowship on mission from the base of their context.

To see these writings, connect with The Baptist Paper at tbponline.org/George-Bullard.

Blessings to you and your ministry!